LIBRARY USE ONLY

**PLEASE USE THIS BOOK
IN THIS AREA**

The art and science of visual illusions

International Library of Psychology

General editor: Max Coltheart
Professor of Psychology, University of London

The art and science of visual illusions

Nicholas Wade

Routledge & Kegan Paul
London, Boston, Melbourne and Henley

First published in 1982
by Routledge & Kegan Paul Ltd
39 Store Street,
London WC1E 7DD,
9 Park Street,
Boston, Mass. 02108, USA,
296 Beaconsfield Parade, Middle Park,
Melbourne 3206, Australia and
Broadway House,
Newtown Road,
Henley-on-Thames,
Oxon RG9 1EN
Set in Press Roman 10 point
and printed in Great Britain by
Redwood Burn Ltd., Trowbridge
Text and illustrations © Nicholas Wade 1982
No part of this book may be reproduced in
any form without permission from the
publisher, except for the quotation of brief
passages in criticism

Library of Congress Cataloging in Publication Data
Wade, Nicholas.
   The art and science of visual illusions.
   (International library of psychology)
   Bibliography: p.
   1. Optical illusions. I. Title. II. Series.
QP495.W2   152.1'48   82-623
ISBN 0-7100-0868-6   AACR2

Dedicated to

109919

Contents

Preface		ix
1	Op Art	1
	1.1 Introduction	1
	1.2 Gestalt grouping principles	3
	1.3 Moiré patterns	35
	1.4 Optical distortions	73
	1.5 After-images and simultaneous contrast	100
	1.6 Grids and checkerboards	106
	1.7 Subjective contours	133
	1.8 Binocular rivalry	151
	1.9 Summary	161
2	Geometrical illusions	162
	2.1 Introduction	162
	2.2 Geometrical optical illusions	163
	2.3 Theories of illusions	184
	2.4 Reversing and impossible figures	189
3	Op-tical illusions	198
	3.1 Introduction	198
	3.2 Op-tical illusions	198
	3.3 Reversing figures	240
	3.4 Stereokinetic effect	256
	3.5 Conclusions	263
Notes		265
Bibliography		277
Index of names		288
Index of subjects		291

Preface

Illusions have fascinated man throughout recorded history. Philosophers have speculated over their causes, charlatans have manipulated them to deceive the naive, and artists have recorded their many instances of occurrence. With such a legacy of interest it is surprising that the scientific study of visual illusions appeared so late. What are called the geometrical optical illusions only received this label in the middle of the nineteenth century, and much work on them has been done by psychologists in the meantime. However, these illusions — which involve distortions of size, shape or orientation — have rarely been used by artists. This is all the more intriguing because a recent movement in art, starting around the early 1960s and concerned specifically with generating optical distortions, has not drawn on the body of geometrical optical illusions studied by psychologists. Rather, these Op Artists have used a variety of visual phenomena that occur constantly in our everyday perception, but which are usually overlooked or ignored. Their skill has been to make these minor aberrations glaringly obvious to us in the paintings and kinetic works they have produced. These aberrations will be discussed in the first chapter, with many illustrative examples of how they can be rendered more readily apparent.

The second chapter deals with the more circumscribed area of geometrical optical illusions as they are studied by psychologists. Indeed, the term itself has a rather archaic ring to it, echoing the mid-nineteenth-century Teutonic desire for precision. More frequently they are referred to as geometrical or spatial illusions, with the term optical describing the broader class of illusions involving 'tricks of the light'. Of course, it can be argued that all perception is illusion and hence the word has little utility. Here illusions refer to the phenomena involving specific and systematic errors of perception which

Preface

occur when sufficient evidence for correct perception is provided. The figures illustrating the geometrical illusions are bland in comparison to those of Op Art. In fact it is a sad feature of visual science that phenomena of interest are reduced to banal simplicity. That is, the one science that should foster the kinship with its sister art does the reverse — there seems to be no room for visual art in visual science. This predilection for pictorial simplicity in representing the geometrical illusions has borne many theoretical fruits though few have been edible. We still do not understand why these distortions occur.

For this reason I have adopted a somewhat different approach. Rather than simplifying the figures yielding geometrical distortions they have been purposely complicated by confounding many different phenomena within a single illustration. More specifically, I have tried to blend the areas of Op Art and geometrical illusions, hence the title of the final chapter, Op-tical Illusions, in which these illustrations are presented.

The aim of this book is to attempt to span the gap between the artists' and the scientists' approach to visual illusions. The areas of Op Art and geometrical illusions are examined separately in the first two chapters and then they are combined in the final one. Wherever possible, I have tried to provide an interpretation of why the particular phenomena under study occur. Paradoxically, this is more difficult in the area of geometrical illusions, which have enjoyed over a century of detailed study, than it is for the bases of Op Art.

The book is primarily illustrative, although it is not without some theoretical intent. All the illustrations have been drawn to demonstrate the particular phenomena under study. Some are titled, as they exist as screen or lithographic prints. The illustrations pose perceptual puzzles which are intended to provoke thought about the nature of perception. They are demonstrations which appeal directly to the richness of the observer's visual experience. No data are given to support statements regarding the designs; the final arbiter is the appearance of the patterns to the viewer.

In trying to bridge the gulf between the science and art of perception it is virtually inevitable that the text will prove unsatisfactory to the psychologist and the illustrations unsatisfactory for the artist. None the less, it is hoped that each group might give some consideration to those parts that might not seem so unsatisfactory.

This book can be treated as a set of illustrations and enjoyed at the purely visual level; but the patterns were designed with theoretical issues in mind, and I believe it is possible to derive insights into theories through pictures. The text develops some of these ideas, as well as providing notes for those wishing to pursue the theoretical points described. The references cited are necessarily selective, but they will provide more detailed discussion on many of the issues discussed here in a more cursory manner.

1 Op Art

1.1 Introduction

In general, artists and scientists are concerned with the same issues — recording, analysing and interpreting the phenomena surrounding us. The subject matter is similar, but the approach differs. The ground rules for art are not clearly defined and it is not readily apparent when any lasting advances have been achieved. Science, on the contrary, has compiled precise procedures for obtaining and evaluating evidence, and major contributions are rapidly appreciated. The price science pays for these is its conservatism — a characteristic not unknown to Established Art, too. Artists have not felt so disposed to adopt the methods or concepts of their predecessors, and this has resulted in a perplexing plethora of styles and movements. One of the movements that had its genesis in the early 1960s has been called Op Art. The label is an abbreviation of Optical Art, because it was considered that the works were dependent upon the optical characteristics of the eye. The founding father is Victor Vasarely, who has been producing works in the Op idiom since the early 1950s.[1] The movement has been more influential within Europe than America, and its history has been chronicled by a number of scholars.[2] The early works, in the 1960s, were predominantly black and white, but now a broader spectrum of colours tends to be applied. The use of black and white does confer certain advantages: the contrast between the lines is at its maximum, which enhances most of the 'optical' effects involved.

What is Op Art? First, it is geometrical and hard-edged. That is, the forms used are precisely defined by sharp edges and the forms themselves tend to be geometrical rather than naturalistic. Second, it has tended to be abstract — involving no representational features —

1

Op Art

though I hope that it will be evident by the end of this chapter that abstraction is not a necessary prerequisite. The aspect of Op Art that distinguishes it from many other forms of geometrical abstraction is its reliance on dramatic or striking visual effects produced by the arrangement of the lines and shapes. The works demand a more immediate interaction with the observer, since the observer's eyes are a vital component of the piece. Of course, it can be said that this applies to all aspects of art appreciation; however, in Op Art the paintings can appear to move and change as a consequence of processes occurring within the visual system itself.

In this chapter Op works will be classified according to the particular visual phenomena that are manipulated when viewing them. That is, rather than describing works in terms of their physical structure — whether two dimensional or three dimensional, whether stationary or kinetic — they will be categorized with regard to the visual process exploited. Moreover, attention will be directed primarily, though not exclusively, to black-and-white Op works. The early impact of Op Art was due in part to a restriction of the paintings to black and white, which enhanced the vibrancy of many of the visual phenomena.

One of the initial stages in the perceptual process involves differentiating a figure from its background and isolating the related parts of the figure. The group of psychologists who attempted to describe these aspects of perceptual organization in most detail were called Gestaltists, because of their emphasis on the holistic nature of perception.[3] These grouping principles have been manipulated within Op Art and examples of them will initiate the illustrative sections of this chapter. There follows a section concerned with superimposed, periodic patterns — called moiré fringes. These have been employed most effectively by Op Artists because the moiré patterns can be generated by several means. For example, the moiré fringes can be stable and stationary as when painted or drawn on a two-dimensional surface or they can be variable and dynamic by separating the two periodic patterns and moving them relative to one another. The remaining sections deal with some specific aspects of vision. Light passing through the eye is distorted slightly due to certain structures like the shape of the eyeball and the lens. Section 1.4 examines the phenomena consequent upon these, particularly those due to astigmatism which causes blurring of lines in some directions but not in others. Intense stimulation by light generates after-images; that is, images which remain visible when the pattern that produced them is no longer present. These are examined in section 1.5, together with simultaneous contrast effects —

phenomena in which the brightness or colour of a surface can be influenced by the nature of its surround. Some related contrast effects can be observed in grids composed of black squares on a white ground or vice versa; in each case illusory dots can be seen at the intersections of the grids, and these are the subject of section 1.6, as are the checkerboard patterns formed by adjacent squares or rectangles of black and white. Section 1.7 deals with the phenomena of subjective contours: those conditions under which a line or an edge is apparent in a display but there is no physical correlate of it. The foregoing phenomena are all visible with a single eye. The last section concerns vision with two eyes, not in terms of their co-operation in yielding stereoscopic depth perception, but with respect to their competition in binocular rivalry. When sufficiently dissimilar images are presented to each eye they are not combined, but alternate in visibility either over the whole field or in local parts of it. Binocular rivalry has not previously been incorporated within the armoury of the Op Artist, but it seems particularly suited for inclusion − constant variations in perception are provided by the operation of the visual system itself without further intervention of the artist or scientist. Under certain circumstances perceptual attenuation can be induced monocularly and patterns favouring such visual variation are also described.

The system of classification has influenced the way in which I have designed the illustrations and the aspects incorporated within them. The designs often elicit more phenomena than the single one specified and these are sometimes, though not always, mentioned. The classification itself was derived from an examination of the corpus of work produced in the area of Op Art, before the illustrations were drawn.[4] I do not wish to suggest that Op Artists have proceeded in this manner. Their manipulation of the phenomena has been at an intuitive rather than at an analytic level. They have used their own perception to guide the development of their art.

1.2 Gestalt grouping principles

The organization of small elements of a larger design has been used by artists through the ages and certainly since the development of Greek mosaics.[5] However, a detailed description of the grouping principles was not given until earlier this century, by the German psychologists, Max Wertheimer, Wolfgang Köhler and Kurt Koffka. They were called the Gestalt school because of their stress on the organizational aspects of perception. They formulated descriptive rules for the perceptual grouping of elements in a larger display.[6] The principles were defined in terms of the stimulus elements rather than any properties of the visual system, although they did argue paradoxically that the perceptual organizations were innate. Grouping in patterns of elements was said to be dependent upon the nearness or proximity of elements, their similarity to one another, whether they were symmetrically arranged or fell along continuous lines. While it will be seen that these principles are by no means simple even at the pictorial level, it is necessary to introduce another more primitive feature before discussing them in more detail. Prior to the organization of elements it is necessary for the elements themselves to be isolated from the background upon which they are placed. Put more generally, a figure or element needs to be segregated from its background. In describing how this process occurred the Gestaltists drew upon the studies of a Danish psychologist called Edgar Rubin.[7] He drew certain designs which accentuated the potential ambiguity between a figure and its background, most notably a pattern that could be seen either as a vase or two profiles facing one another, rather like the central portion of *1.2.2*.* The significance of Rubin's demonstration is that it is difficult to see both aspects — vase and faces — simultaneously: rather the appearance tends to switch between the two possible interpretations. Normally, a figure is defined by having closed contours, with its boundaries separating it from the less structured and larger background. Thus, *1.2.1* will probably appear like a conventional goblet; it is stable and initially unambiguous but it turns Rubin's notion on its head: turning the figure upside-down will yield two swan-necked profiles! Once this possibility has been appreciated the inverted faces can vie with the goblet for attention; i.e., the percept can alternate between the black goblet on a white background or two inverted white faces against a black background. The figure defines the background and vice versa. This characteristic does not apply to *1.2.2*, since the background for both the vase and faces is black, yet it remains difficult to perceive the alternatives together. A similar principle is operating in *1.2.3*, in which more conventional Rubin figures are juxtaposed in opposing contrasts. If black is taken as the background then faces should be seen in some parts at the same time as vases in others, though this seldom occurs. Of course, one of the processes determining which parts of the pattern are perceived concerns where the eyes are directed. Most spatial detail is extracted in and around the

* Italicized numbers refer to illustrations.

fovea, along the optical axis of the eye, and other parts are not resolved as clearly. Those parts fixated are more likely to be perceived as dominant, and a change in fixation can be associated with an alternation in perception. Frequently this is what is meant by 'directing attention' to some particular part of a pattern or scene. However, it is unlikely to be the only factor involved in figure-ground organization because perceptual alternations are reported when patterns are stabilized on the retina, so that they move with the eye.[8] That is, when the eye moves in order to fixate another part of the pattern then the pattern moves with the eye to remain in the same relative position. One of the consequences of employing this technique is that the pattern usually becomes invisible after a few seconds, which indicates how important our eye movements are for constantly changing the pattern of stimulation on the retina, thereby maintaining the visibility of objects.

The contrast of the elements in figure-ground organization can also be manipulated, as in *1.2.4*. Although the goblets are half-black and half-white they can still be segregated from their backgrounds. Such segregation can itself be ambiguous, as in the case of *1.2.5* and *1.2.6*, where heads are superimposed upon one another and definitions of the colour of figure and ground no longer apply. None the less, it is possible to extract the figures from such relatively complex embedding. It seems as though the fragmentary clues there are regarding the figures are used to predict the different parts.[9] If the predictions are confirmed within the pattern then we sustain an hypothesis about the figure, if not then we need to formulate alternative interpretations. In these examples the initial hypotheses are fairly obvious, whereas in many of the other instances that occur later in the section they will not be so straightforward.

Extraction of a figure from its background might well be the initial process in perception, but it is by no means a simple one. It involves much more than segregating parts of the pattern that are enclosed or have the same colour. Rather it would seem to be dependent on the predictive use of fragmentary evidence that is the hallmark of more complex perceptual processes.

In many artistic works a figure can be defined or separated from its background by a line. Indeed, the importance of the drawn line, no matter how simple, has been stressed by many artists both in their pictorial and written work.[10] In much the same context, the Gestalt psychologists have provided demonstrational support for their grouping principles with outline drawings. For example, *1.2.7* is made up of six figures which illustrate Gestalt principles of perceptual organization; that the demonstrations work has been determined from the spontaneous descriptions given by observers when looking at the configurations. *1.2.7a* is said to look like three columns or three pairs of lines; although there are many alternatives to this description (e.g. two sets of three vertical lines) they are rarely given. The elements of the configuration are the equally sized dots but these tend to be grouped to form vertical lines. The lines are similar in length and orientation, but they differ with regard to their distance or *proximity* from one another. The lines tend to be grouped in terms of the proximity to their neighbours. In *1.2.7b* the dots tend to be described as three columns of black and white dots. Although all the dots are equally spaced, so that proximity cannot be operating, they are grouped according to their *similarity*. Other things being equal, similar elements within a large configuration will be related perceptually. The organizing principles rarely operate in isolation, more frequently they complement or counteract one another. For example, in *1.2.7c* the dots are typically described as forming two symmetrical triangles, of black and white dots. Here the *symmetry* principle is operating together with similarity but against proximity. The dots in *1.2.7d* are most commonly said to form two intersecting curved lines rather than, say, two V-shapes meeting at their points. This organizing principle is referred to as *good continuation*: we perceive elements as maintaining some approximate continuity of direction rather than changing direction abruptly. Some shapes like circles, squares and triangles were referred to by the Gestaltists as *good figures* in the sense that they have a figural identity which cannot be reduced perceptually to simpler components. Thus they would say that a square has an identity that is more than the sum of its four sides. Even patterns of dots following such curves, like the circles in *1.2.7e*, display this 'goodness of figure'; they also illustrate another Gestalt principle, that of *closure*. In each of the four circular patterns a dot is missing from the regular sequence: patterns that have small segments missing tend to be completed perceptually, thus displaying the principle of closure. Finally, in *1.2.7f* the various organizing principles operate in a way to conceal aspects of the pattern. It would frequently be described as a diamond flanked by two vertical lines, but rarely as a letter W above a letter M. In this instance we are dealing with *embedded figures*, which are hidden by the operation of the grouping rules to yield alternative perceptions.

It is a fascinating paradox that the Gestaltists, who created a good descriptive classification of grouping principles, did not provide the best examples of perceptual grouping. Rather, artists working with freer and more intuitive organizational principles have filled this pictorial niche, and this applies particularly to various Op Artists.[11] Before providing alternative and more complex illustrations of grouping a further point should be noted: in the absence of any stimulus features for proximity, similarity, etc., grouping still tends to be imposed on a pattern of elements. *1.2.8* consists of a matrix of evenly spaced, black dots which form several changing subgroupings upon detailed viewing: the dots may group into squares, rows, columns or more complex combinations. Accordingly, as in the case of figure-ground segregation, perceptual organization cannot be reduced to stimulus features alone. Consideration must also be given to organizational processes within the brain.

The remaining illustrations in this section incorporate the grouping principles, acting alone or in concert, but within designs more closely akin to the Op than the psychological tradition of representation. The initial examples (*1.2.9* to *1.2.17*) are relatively simple, and the reader should readily discern the principles at play in each one. There follow many instances of embedded figures in more complex designs.

As mentioned above, the Gestalt psychologists discussed the problems of figure segregation in complex patterns, particularly when certain of the grouping principles operate to hide or camouflage a shape. Many experiments were conducted to study such embedded figures, but again the stimuli used were relatively simple outline drawings.[12] In general, it is possible to use some of the grouping principles to render it difficult to segregate particular features of a pattern. For instance, *1.2.18* to *1.2.22* are all comprised of intersecting circles, with lines radiating through points of intersection of the circles. However, the normal figure-ground contrast relations between the circles and their surrounds have been contravened, so that a given circle encloses a variety of black and white forms. It is relatively easy to segregate the central circles but it becomes more difficult for the outer ones, and extremely so for the more complex intersections like *1.2.21* and *1.2.22*. The next two illustrations (*1.2.23* and *1.2.24*) employ circles either to mask their own form or that of other, less abstract, figures.

Symmetry can frequently mask the existence of other forms, as shown simply in *1.2.25*. The outlines of the two asymmetrical figures on the left and right are superimposed in the central pair. None the less, the symmetrical forms dominate perceptually, and this is enhanced by the black 'background' against which the central white forms are contrasted. The component figures are rendered less immediately evident in *1.2.26* to *1.2.29*.

The principle of good continuation defines forms that might otherwise be lost in *1.2.30* to *1.2.32*. In fact the first two reflect the same form, which can probably be discerned if the patterns are viewed from a distance or with blurred vision. The form is incorporated precisely within *1.2.31*, but at right angles to the abstraction of it; that is, the figure defines and masks its own abstraction. In *1.2.32* red herrings have been introduced into the design in the form of irrelevant contours to suggest continuity along lines that do not define the underlying form.

Circular designs offer a particularly potent means of embedding figures, and they can be extremely difficult to 'decode'. For instance, *1.2.33* is composed of facial profiles, alternating in direction, which are masked by the circular symmetry of the overlapping elements. Moreover, the good continuation between these circular elements operates against that for the profiles. Even with knowledge of the exact form the profiles follow they can prove testing to segregate. The theme of profiles is pursued in *1.2.34* and *1.2.35*, but here heads are defined by the profiles, which are seen in their entirety in the forms emanating from the heads. (The source of origin of the heads is itself not arbitrary, corresponding to the Cartesian pineal minds in *1.2.34* and the eyes in *1.2.35*!)

It is hoped that the illustrations can have an aesthetic appeal independently of the components incorporated within them. This point is especially pertinent for the remaining designs, which can be viewed without pondering over the hidden elements. Indeed, *1.2.36* almost defies disentanglement with full comprehension of the defined form.

The final three circular examples all contain central clues to the visual conundra they pose, which clues are also suggested by their titles. *Torson* (*1.2.37*) depicts a rotating torso with circumferential heads of the same form as the central one. *Legacy* (*1.2.38*) similarly rotates legs, with the central feet repeated around the circumference. However, with *Forfeit* (*1.2.39*) there is a visual puzzle in the centre, the clues for which are provided around the extremities of the circle. As the title describes, there are four feet superimposed in the centre having the same dimensions as those on the circumference; they do not initially appear the same because the overlapping feet in the centre are not uniformly black or white, but vary with the geometry of their rotations. The circumferential feet are attached to legs that radiate from the centre, but alternate in direction to produce the overlapping patterns. In all these cases the circular symmetries generate organizations of their own which mask the component contours, and it is only with considerable cognitive persistence that the latter may come to light.

To repeat a point made above, if these illustrations have achieved their purpose, their appeal will extend beyond the pictorial puzzles they pose. Such puzzles could easily have been presented in simpler forms, as they have been throughout the history of visual science. Their incorporation in complex patterns might prove more pleasing visually and might also correspond a little more closely to the complex problems posed by the objects scattered around our real environment.

The last illustration (*1.2.40*) is also a repetition or an echo of the initial concern with figure-ground segregation. Rubin's vase/faces is presented again, but this time without any abrupt contrast effects to segregate the figure from the background.

1.2.3

1.2.4

1.2.5

1.2.6

1.2.7

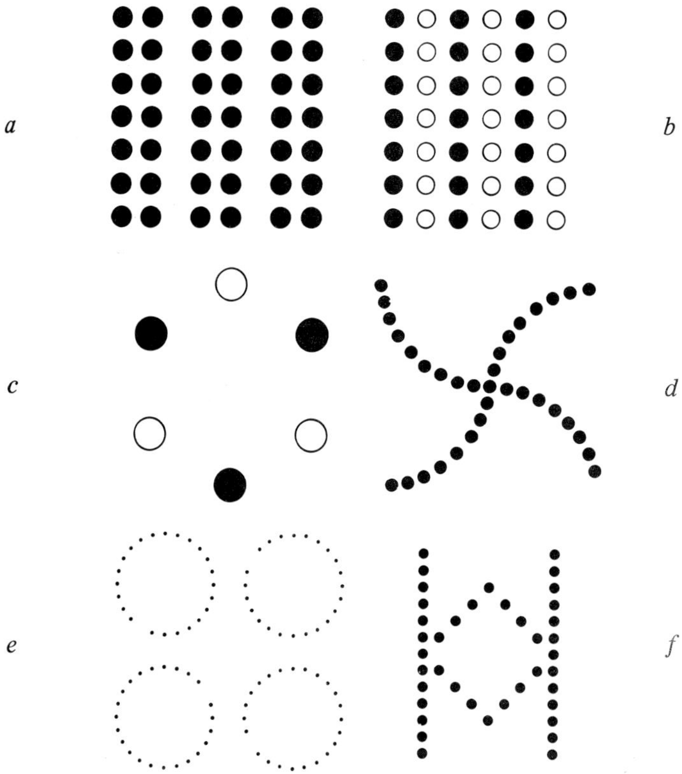

a *b*

c *d*

e *f*

1.2.8

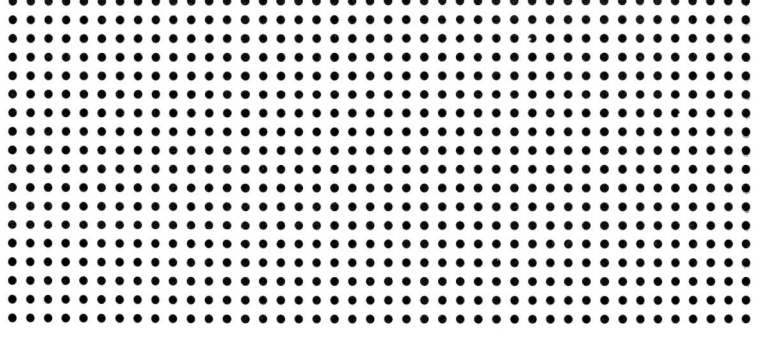

13

1.2.9

1.2.10

1.2.11

1.2.12

15

1.2.13

1.2.14

1.2.15

1.2.16

1.2.17

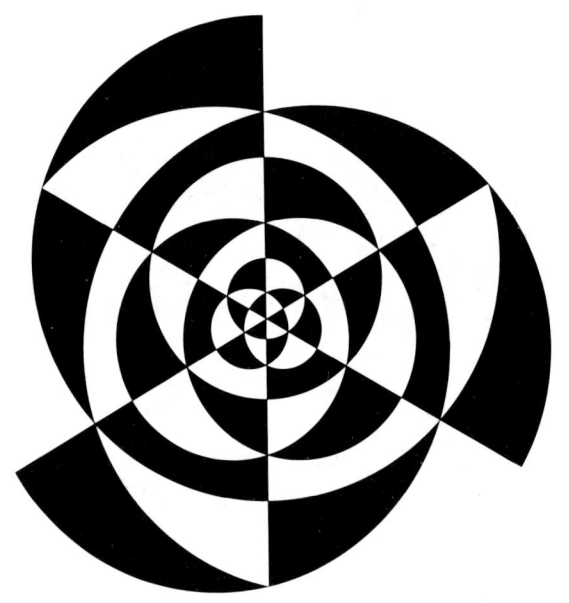

1.2.18

1.2.19

1.2.20

1.2.21

1.2.22

1.2.23

1.2.24

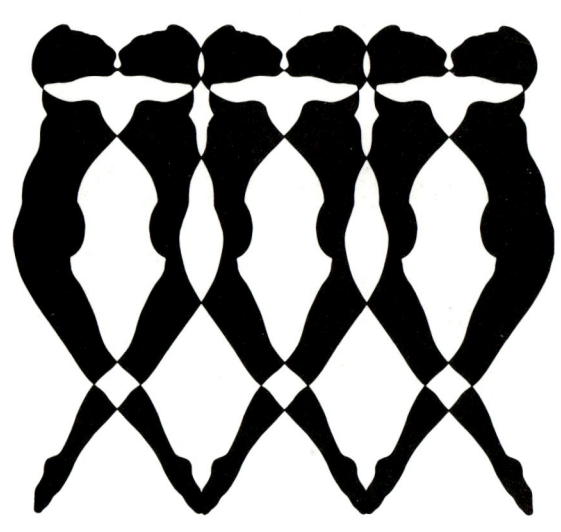

1.2.27

1.2.28

1.2.30

1.2.31

1.2.32

1.2.33

1.2.34

1.2.36

1.2.37 *Torson*

1.2.38 *Legacy*

1.2.39 *Forfeit*

1.2.40

1.3.1   Op Art

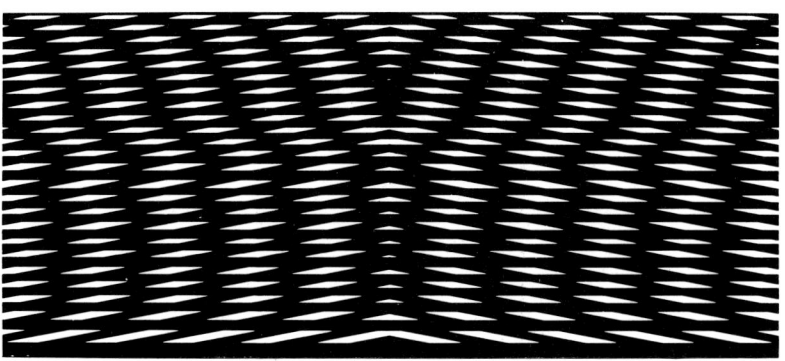

1.3 Moiré patterns

Moiré patterns are produced when two geometrically periodic patterns are superimposed.[13] They occur constantly in everyday perception, most commonly when lace curtains overlap – the wavy patterns seen are the moiré fringes produced by the interaction of the dominant weaves of the material. The term moiré itself derives from the French name for watered silk. When the two component patterns are the same they need to be displaced relative to one another in order to produce moiré patterns. For simple figures, like equally spaced parallel lines (referred to also as gratings), the characteristics of the moiré fringes can be described mathematically.[14]

The first example of a moiré pattern (*1.3.1*) is closely related to the previous illustration, but here the vase and faces are defined by moiré fringes. The component patterns are sets of parallel lines and the curvature in the fringes results from slight variations in the line spacing; the sum of all the small changes defines the facial profiles.

If all the lines in the two gratings are equally spaced then rotation of one will produce moiré fringes that bisect them, as in *1.3.2*. The relative inclination of the gratings determines the separation of the adjacent fringes: *1.3.3* is made up of a vertical grating superimposed upon others at slightly different inclinations, so that more fringes are produced at the top and bottom of the design than in the central region. One of the features that might have been noticed in the previous examples is that the black areas of the moiré fringes (where there is maximum displacement between the lines of the component patterns)

35

look 'blacker' than the other parts of the black lines; conversely, the central white areas (where the overlap is minimal) seem 'whiter' than the neighbouring white areas. In both instances it is likely that some degree of simultaneous contrast (see section 1.5) is operating to increase the distinctiveness of the darker and lighter areas. Such contrast effects are usually attributed to interactions between nerve cells, called lateral inhibition:[15] neurons lying next to one another exert mutual inhibition so that differences in the pattern of stimulation are enhanced. They can also be seen in the moiré curves of *1.3.4*; in fact the shape of the curve itself mirrors the response characteristics of visual neurons held to be involved in lateral inhibition.[16]

Figures *1.3.5* to *1.3.15* represent more complex moiré fringes that either define forms by means of variable line spacing or augment the figural components present in one underlying design. For example, in *1.3.7* the moiré fringes correspond to the sides of a figure that is represented in the centre. This ghostly form is defined by slight increases in the line thickness, and these small changes are accentuated perceptually.

Delightfully intricate moiré patterns can be produced by means of a mechanical device generally called an harmonograph.[17] This is a contrivance that moves a platform beneath a stationary pen, and examples of its operation can be seen in *1.3.16* to *1.3.22*. The first three consist of simple patterns superimposed on one other, whereas the next three show the complex trajectories that generate moiré patterns within them. The final illustration shows a facetious example that is beyond the moiré fringe!

All the moiré patterns illustrated so far are static and two-dimensional. Although the designs might have appeared very active visually, the moiré fringes remained in fixed positions. Two techniques can be employed to generate dynamic moiré patterns. The first involves superimposing and moving a transparency of one periodic pattern over another.[18] For example, moving the transparency* of *1.3.23* horizontally over the pattern will produce vertical moiré fringes which change at different frequencies — this makes it look as though the adjacent horizontal bands are moving in opposite directions. Tilting the transparency produces parallel fringes, but more impressive moirés result from rotating the overlay of *1.3.24* — because of the increasing separation of the lines the fringes are curved. Superimposing the transparency from *1.3.23* on this underlay will yield another family of

---

* The transparent overlay patterns can be found in the envelope attached to the inside of the back cover. These are numbered according to the designs with which they should be used.

curves.

Following the pioneering research of Lord Rayleigh,[19] over a century ago, on the mathematical characteristics of moiré fringes, they have been employed to determine the evenness of spacings within gratings. Any slight departures from regularity are more readily visible in the moiré fringes of superimposed patterns than in the patterns themselves.[20] In the case of gratings the irregularities show themselves in slight departures from parallelism in the fringes. Rather than trying to overcome this problem it can be manipulated so that the irregularities are not random, but define a pattern. That is, a figure can be embedded in the slight irregularities of a grating so that it will only emerge when a regular pattern is superimposed upon it. This is illustrated in *1.3.25*. The horizontal lines of the underlay are clearly irregular, but it comes as a surprise that these irregularities define forms when the curved transparency is superimposed on it. With a little imagination it may be possible to see outward- and inward-facing profiles in the upper and lower halves of the pattern. The curves are evenly spaced and the slight variations in the horizontal lines are sufficient to define the profiles in the moiré fringes. Moreover, since the curvature increases towards the sides of the transparency the moiré fringes become more densely packed and more nearly straight and vertical. The faces are most easily seen in the centre where it might even prove possible to produce a Rubin vase/faces in the lower half!

The moiré fringes produced by moving the transparencies are dynamic but remain two-dimensional. An ingenious method of introducing depth into such designs has been developed by the artist Ludwig Wilding.[21] He uses vertically striped backgrounds located at different depths that are viewed through a regular vertical grating (made of black elastic attached to the front of the frame). Vertical moiré fringes result from the interaction of the regular grating with those of different spacings in the background design. What proves so intriguing about these works is that the relative positioning of the moiré fringes is different in each eye. (Such differences in the two retinal images are referred to as disparities.) The horizontal disparities in the vertical moiré fringes yield a compelling impression of relative depth within the design, and this apparent depth itself changes as the observer approaches or recedes from the work (as this changes the retinal disparities).

Some approximation to this depth effect can be observed in *1.3.23*. If the regular grating of the transparency is held steadily about 1 cm above the underlay (which has varied line spacing) then the relative positions of the vertical moiré fringes in the horizontal bands will be different for each eye, and the bands might appear in different depth planes.

Similar depth effects can be produced with all the linear designs (*1.3.23* to *1.3.29*), but most strongly in *1.3.27* and *1.3.29* (which have very fine parallel lines). Holding the transparency above the design so as to produce vertical or near vertical fringes gives a strong impression of a surface in depth. When this does not occur it could be that the orientations of the moiré fringes differ by too great a degree for them to be combined binocularly. (The difference can readily be checked by closing each eye in turn and noting the configurations of the moiré fringes.) With large differences in the patterns presented to each eye we tend to see either one or the other at a particular moment or complex combinations of the two and the perceived pattern changes constantly. This phenomenon is called binocular rivalry (see section 1.8).

The complexity of the moiré fringes increases with the introduction of curvature into the component designs, as can be seen in *1.3.30* to *1.3.32*. Even when the transparencies are placed directly upon the underlay, an impression of three dimensionality in the waves can be assisted by slight movement to and fro: the fringes so produced suggest the shading that would be seen on a moving wave.

Radiating lines, when displaced, yield curved fringes that are symmetrical around the centres (*1.3.33*) — rather like the petals of a flower. When the radiating lines zig-zag, as in *1.3.34*, lateral movement of the transparency yields curves which look like parts of spirals. Reversing the transparency, so that the lines are in opposing directions, and rotating it gives the impression of parts rotating concentrically in opposite directions: the whole design can appear insubstantial and fluid. Similar effects can be seen in radiating curved lines (*1.3.35*): the curves define a circle at their extremity, although they are facially radial. When concentric circles are superimposed the moiré fringes radiate from their centres (*1.3.36* and *1.3.37*), which is precisely the reverse of those produced by radiating patterns.

A further variation that has been played on the moiré theme incorporates independently moving parts suspended in front of some periodic pattern. Jesus Raphael Soto has achieved remarkable effects by suspending straight or curved rods in front of horizontal gratings: when the rods are set in slow periodic motion they interact both with the other rods and with the background stripes.[22]

The final design in this section, *Op Eye* (*1.3.38*), embodies several of the aspects mentioned above — radiating lines and parallels varying in width and spacing. It also encompasses various of the phenomena to be discussed in the following sections. For instance, viewing the centre of the printed pattern alone, without the overlay, results in some distortions that appear similar to those produced with the overlay — rosette-like petals that seem to encircle the centre and move with it. These effects are due to some of the optical characteristics of the eye, which are discussed in the next section.

1.3.2

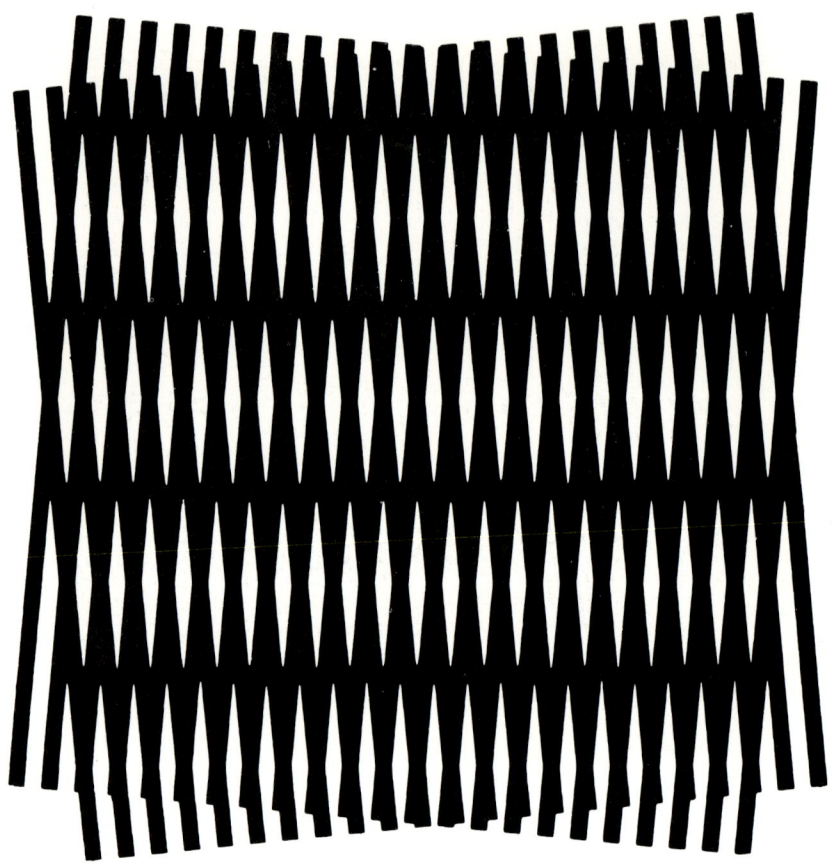

40

1.3.3

1.3.4

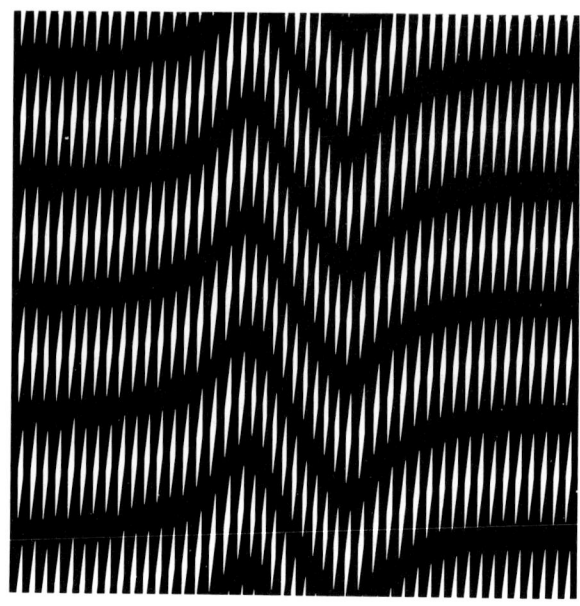

1.3.5

1.3.6

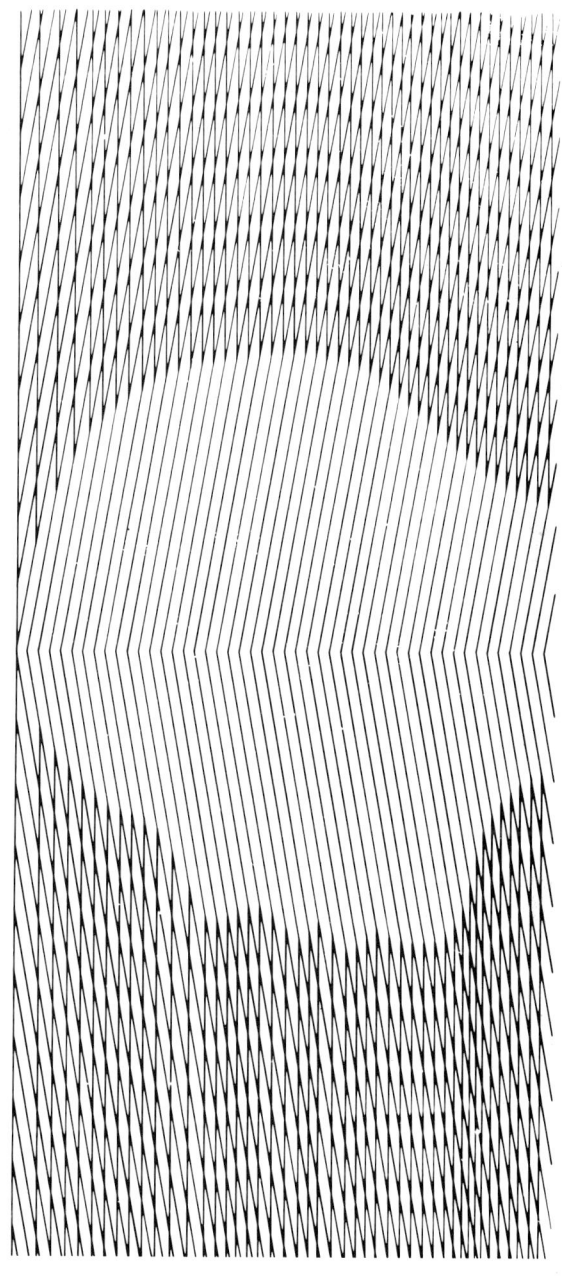

1.3.7

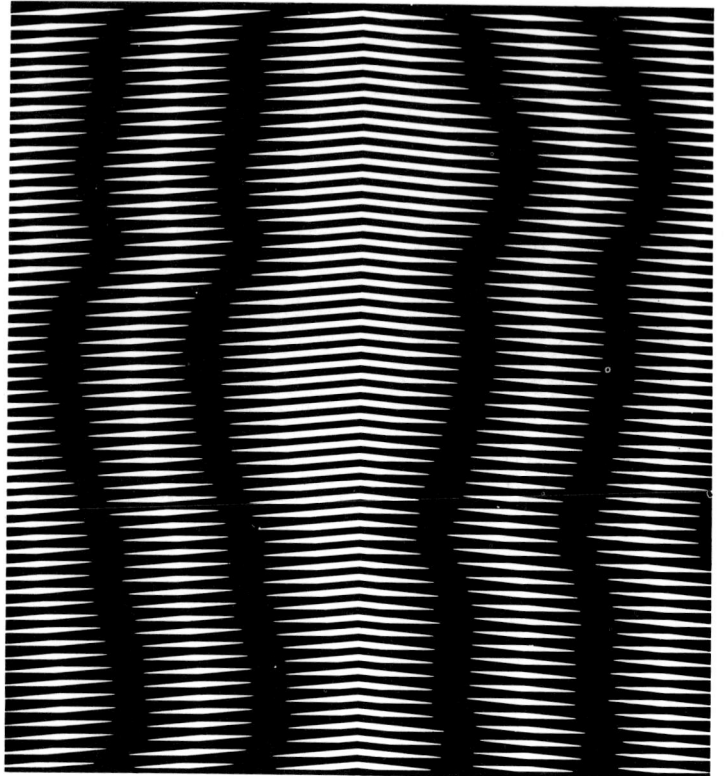

1.3.8

1.3.10

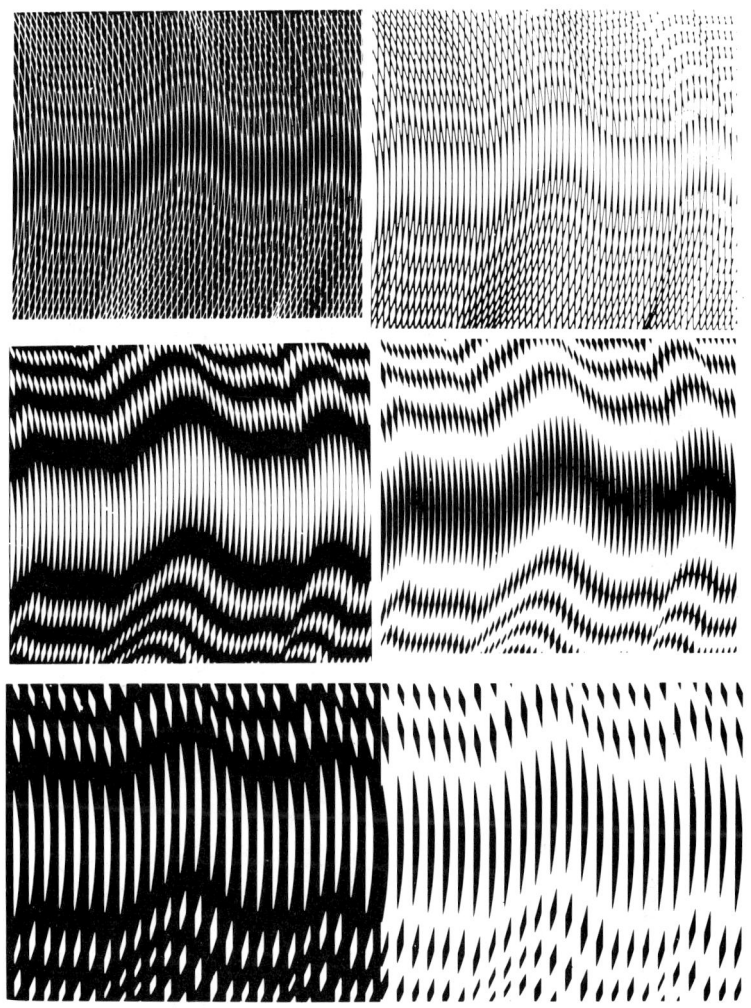

1.3.12

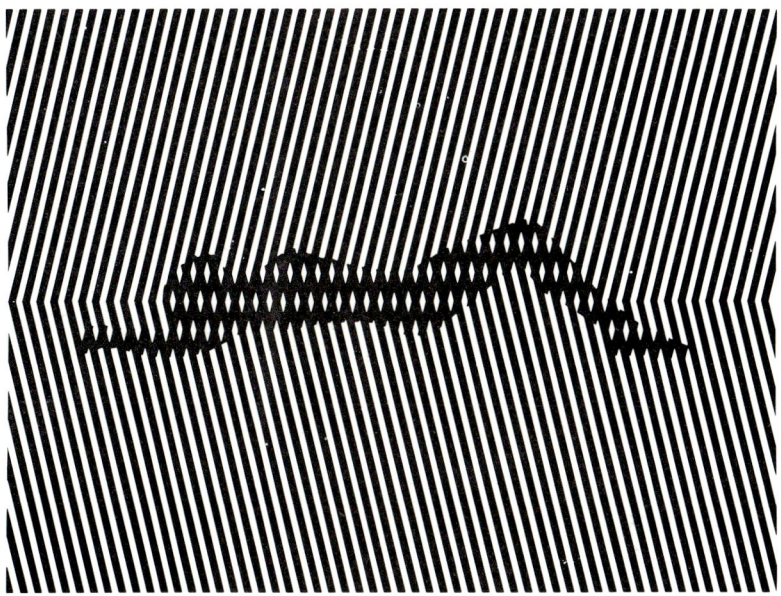

1.3.13

1.3.14

1.3.15

1.3.16

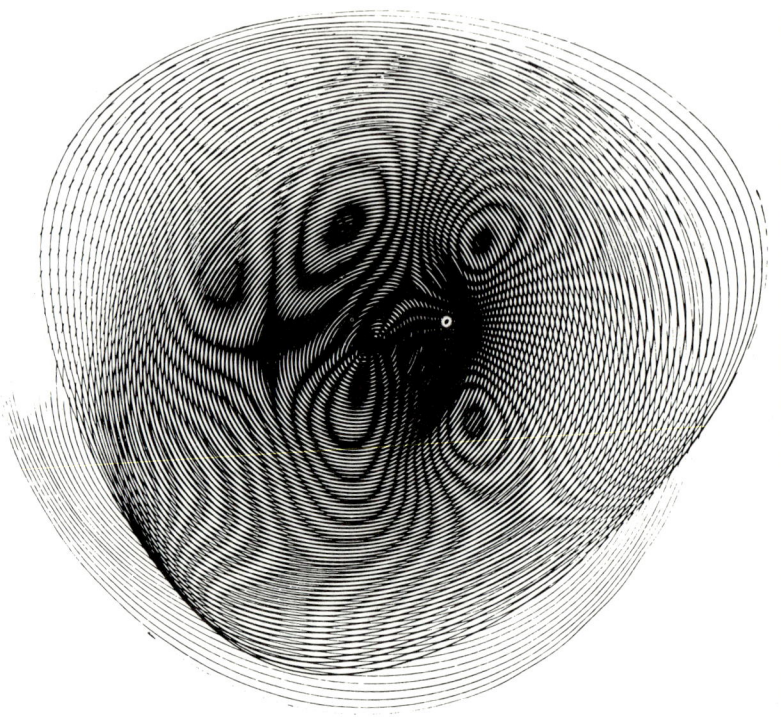

1.3.17

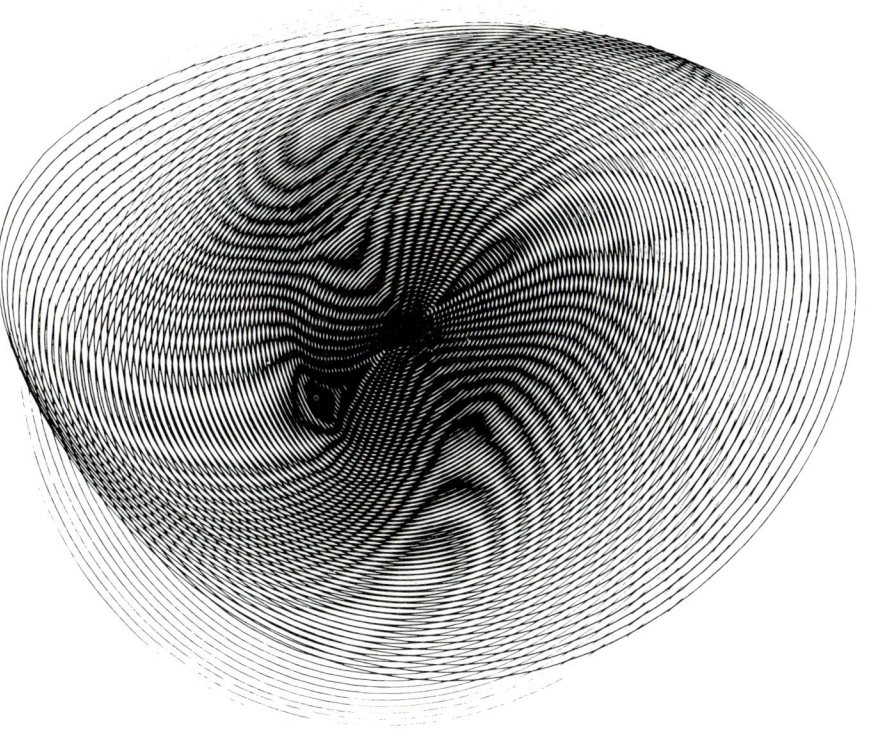

1.3.18

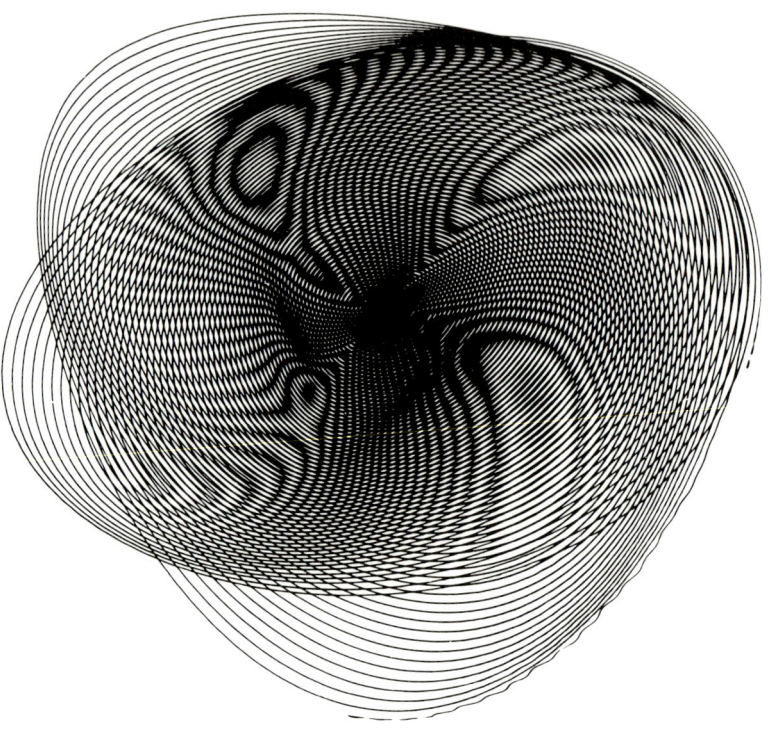

1.3.19

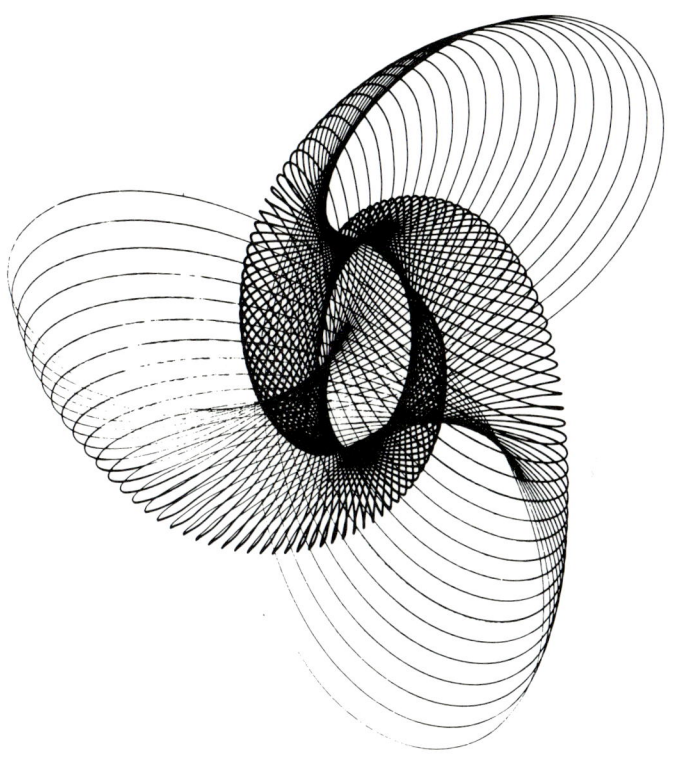

1.3.20

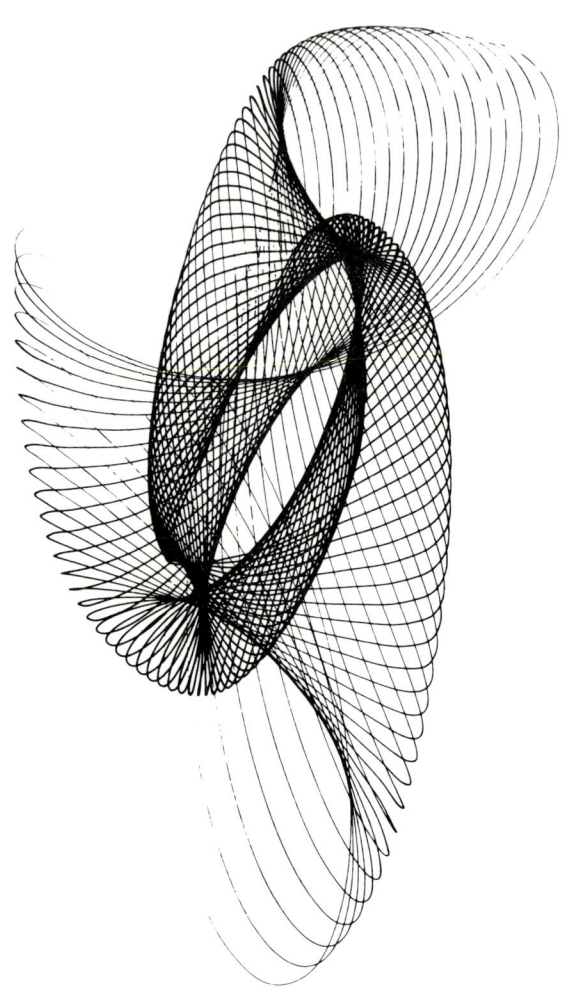

1.3.21

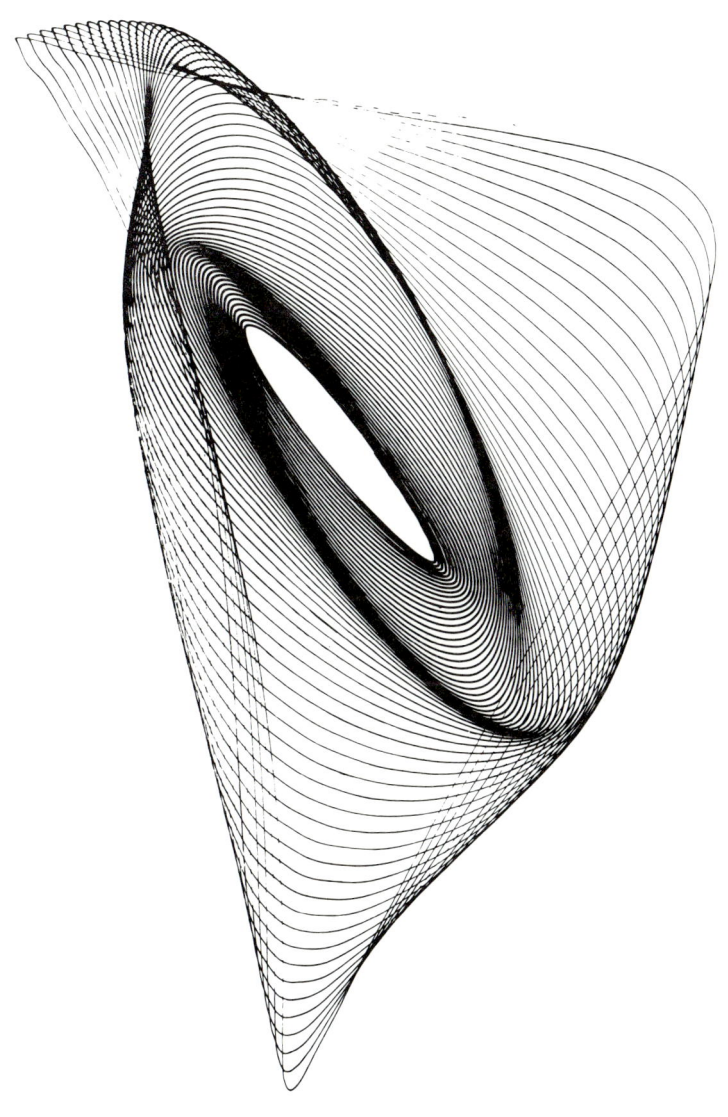

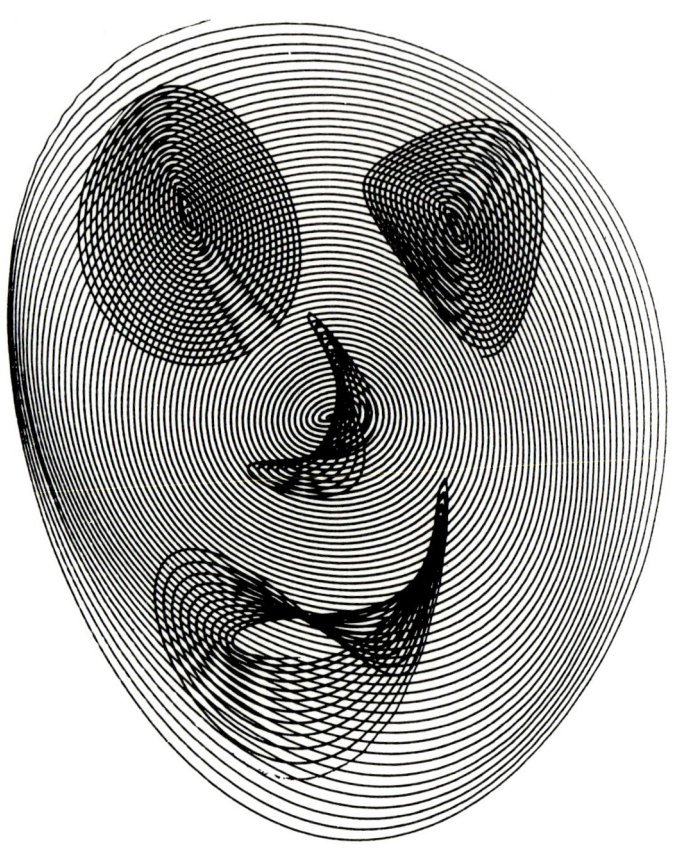

1.3.23

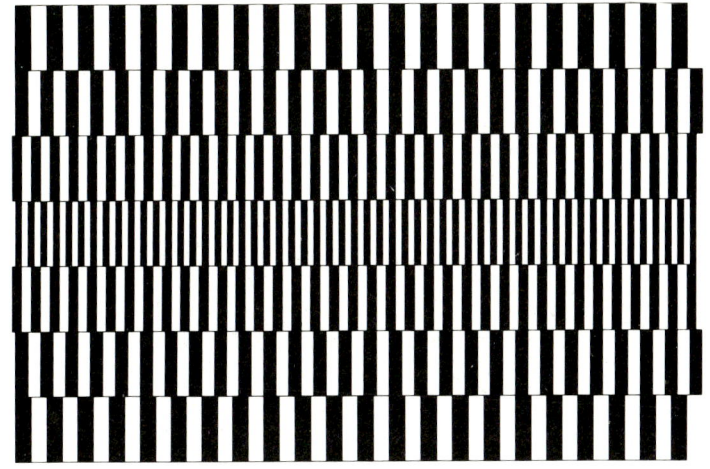

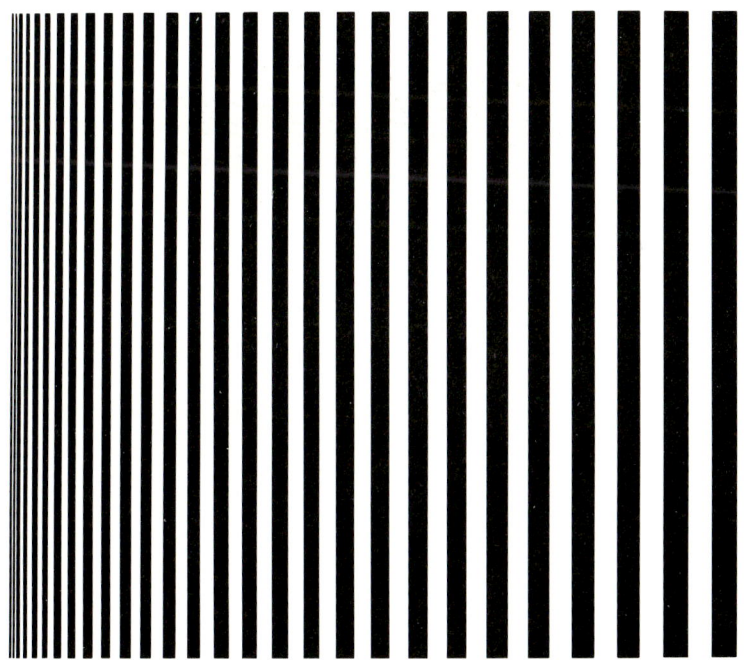

1.3.24

1.3.25

1.3.26 *Linear Contrast*

1.3.27 *Astigmat*

1.3.28 *Op Art*

1.3.29 *Subjectively Contoured*

1.3.30 *Lateral Interaction*

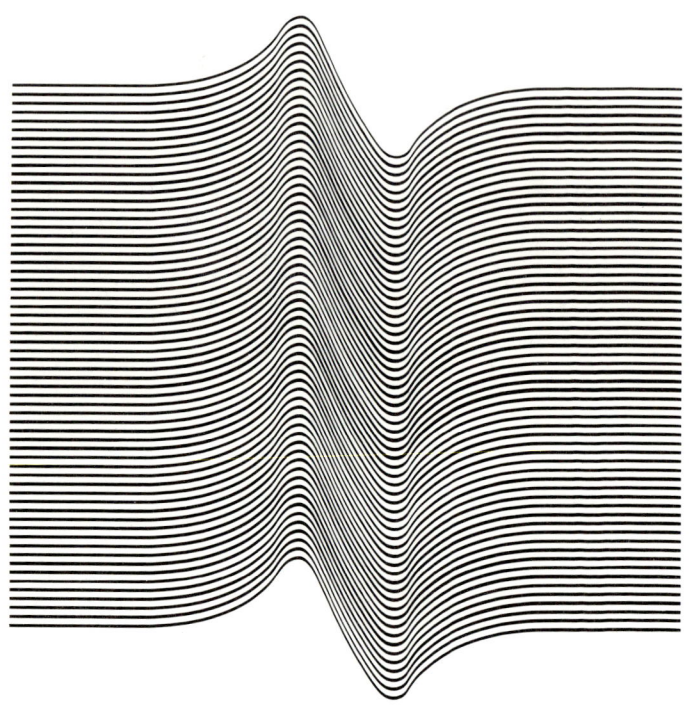

1.3.31 *Bather*

1.3.32

1.3.34

1.3.35

1.3.37 *Playboy*

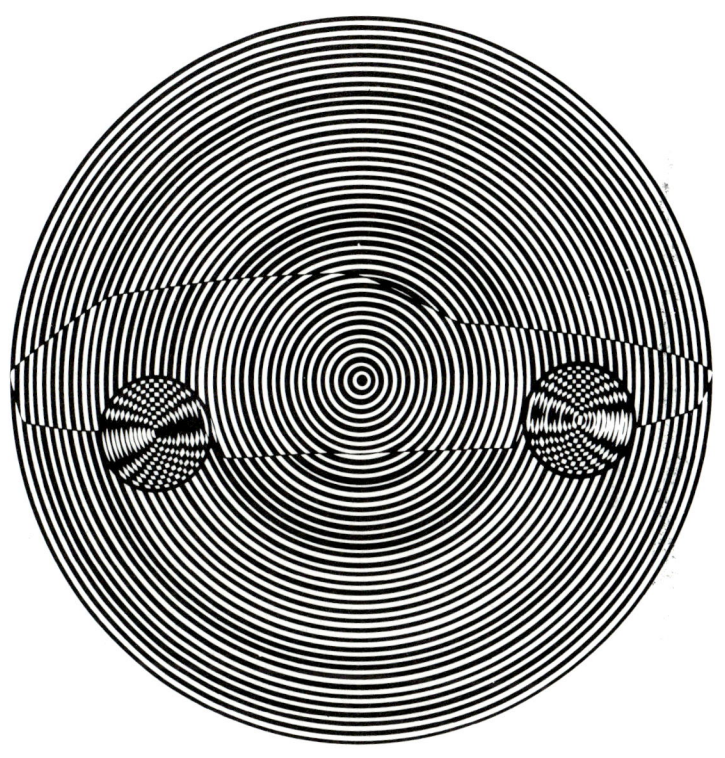

1.3.38 *Op Eye*

1.4 Optical distortions

The radiating lines at the centre of *Op Eye* produce distortions that have circular features. Contrariwise, the concentric circular patterns in *Playboy* (*1.3.37*) may generate radiating 'propellers' or 'spokes' after viewing for a little while. In both cases the distortions themselves are not stable, but appear to pulsate or shimmer. These phenomena can be seen in the concentric circles of *1.4.1*: not only are 'spokes' produced but they appear to rotate also, particularly when the eyes are moved. Thus, here is a series of patterns which are actually stationary but have the appearance of movement within them, even if the eyes are kept as still as possible. Distortions and movement are characteristics of all the designs in this section, and they all share certain stimulus features: they are comprised of fine lines which are densely spaced (of high spatial frequency) and varying in orientation. The orientation changes can be of straight line elements, as in the case of *1.4.2*, where the width of the radiating lines increases with the distance from the centre. The appearance is one of blurred, swirling rings which revolve around the centres of the rays.

The distortions occur in a direction perpendicular to the main lines of the pattern — they are radial for concentric circles and circular for radiating lines. At one time it was considered that the involuntary eye movements, referred to in section 1.2, produced these distortions: when the eyes move in one direction the image of the lines perpendicular to that direction is blurred much more than those lying in the same directions as the eye movement. This can readily be demonstrated by moving the concentric circular pattern (*1.4.1*) vertically or horizontally: vertical movement blurs the horizontal lines with the resulting impression of horizontal spokes (formed from the clearly resolved vertical arcs), and horizontal movement has the reverse effect. While such blurring undoubtedly occurs during eye movements this is unlikely to be the only process involved.[23] Rather, the basis lies in a minor muscular instability within the eye, associated with the mechanism of accommodation. Whenever an object is fixated the light entering the eye requires focusing on the retina, somewhat like focusing a camera. However, in the case of a camera the lens is of fixed curvature and it is moved towards or away from the plane of the film. In the eye focusing, or accommodation, is performed by adjusting the curvature of the crystalline lens within the eye. This adjustment is possible because of certain muscles surrounding the lens — when they contract the curvature of the lens is increased enabling focusing upon nearer objects.

73

One of the consequences of old age is that the lens becomes less flexible and it is more difficult to focus on near objects, although visibility of distant objects poses no problems.[24]

When the eye does not have spherical refracting surfaces the light from lines of different orientations will not be focused in the same plane: either, say, vertical or horizontal lines will be focused sharply and the other orientations will be blurred. This condition is called regular astigmatism, and it will be discussed in more detail later in this section. There is another form of astigmatism which is more closely related to the distortions visible in the figures above; this is called transient astigmatism. Unlike regular astigmatism it is not caused directly by aspects of the optical surfaces of the eye, but by the muscles that control the curvature of the lens. When these muscles contract they do not do so evenly around the lens so that the curvature of the lens varies in different orientations. This results in lines in some orientations appearing sharply in focus and others look blurred.[25] The axes of the clearly defined and blurred lines themselves change, so generating the impression of movement in the patterns viewed, like the rotating spokes in *1.4.1*. When viewing everyday scenes such a small amount of blurring would not be noticed. However, the following patterns have been designed specifically to exploit these minor aberrations in optical image formation. Thus, the differential clarity and motion that occurs in the illustrations is due to these minute and transient variations in the curvature of the lens. They can be seen as more stable patterns if they are viewed through an artificial pupil, like a small pinhole in a piece of black paper. The patterns will look dimmer but they will not appear to be so blurred or to move about as much.[26] An artificial pupil restricts the path of light to the area around the optical axis, where the optical aberrations are least.

The designs are grouped according to the characteristics of the component lines. For instance, figures *1.4.3* to *1.4.6* all contain linear radiating elements. In the first two the eye theme is varied, with shapes defined by changes in contrast — as is also the case in *1.4.5*. The designs are at their most active, visually, around the centres where the lines are at their finest: swirling patterns of dots appear to be rotating around the centres but it is not possible to determine readily the direction in which they are moving. Rotation is also a feature evident upon viewing *1.4.6*, particularly in the four circles seen peripherally. Moreover, the zig-zagging lines themselves seem to change position. Figures *1.4.7* to *1.4.9* all consist of radiating curves. *Chrysanthemum* (*1.4.7*) demonstrates clearly how the visual activity is most pronounced in the parts

Op Art

containing finer lines, as at the points of inflection on the curves. There is also a strong impression of depth in the figure, with curves defining humps or hollows. However, the depth is itself somewhat paradoxical as the contours defining a hump on one side define a hollow on the other! In perceptual parlance this would be called an 'impossible object', as the drawing depicts the depth features of an object that could not be realized in three dimensions (see section 2.4). The depth impressions are more difficult to elicit with the contours of a natural form (*1.4.8*), although both this and *Reflections* (*1.4.9*) are extremely vibrant.

Figures *1.4.10* to *1.4.17* utilize curvature to modulate both line orientation and thickness, which produce blurring and movement in the pattern. When the curves are arranged vertically the apparent motion is horizontal and vice versa. Again strong depth effects can be seen in the patterns, but here the depth is ambiguous rather than paradoxical as in *Chrysanthemum*. That is, a particular wave is ambiguous in so far as it could correspond to a hump or a hollow, but the same wave does not define both states simultaneously. Some of the illustrations contain figurative forms that are fairly readily discernible, but some are more difficult to detect, like the reclining figures occurring throughout *Bali Dancers* (*1.4.17*).

The final group are composed of straight line elements varying in orientation. In *1.4.18* only two orientations are present, 45° and 135°, and these are arranged in the form of concentric squares. A given 'square' consists of lines in one of these orientations alone. The effects of transient astigmatism render the adjacent squares either sharply in focus or fuzzy, and when the axis of astigmatism changes the whole pattern appears to pulsate. The greater intensity of such 'pulsation' can be seen by fixating a particular part and noting that the area around the fixation point is more stable than those projecting more peripherally. Vertical and horizontal lines are present in *1.4.19* in addition to the obliques, whereas both line thickness and orientation are varied in *1.4.20*. Figural elements are also incorporated in this design, as with *1.4.21* and *1.4.22*. *The Model* (*1.4.21*) generates marked variation in the sharpness of the four oblique quadrants; it is also a visual parody of model-building in cognitive psychology, where boxes and arrows are considered to represent processes of perception and thinking. *Op-position* (*1.4.22*) uses the figural components to define the dimensions of the concentric rectangles; in addition to their visual dynamics they create strong depth impressions, which are themselves ambiguous — there could be tunnels or pyramids producing those patterns.

Transient astigmatism and the distorting effects it produces are rarely noticed in our everyday perception. The same cannot be said for those having marked regular astigmatism.[27] If the shape of the eyeball departs appreciably from being spherical then lines in certain orientations will almost always be blurred on the retina. This can be corrected optically by the prescription of cylindrical lenses. However, most of us have a small degree of regular astigmatism that does not warrant optical correction, and this makes either vertical or horizontal lines blurred in most cases.[28] For instance, the vertical and horizontal lines in *1.4.23* might not appear equally clear; one orientation might seem more sharply defined and blacker than the other, which might be slightly blurred. If the book is rotated by 90° so that the lines which were vertical on the retina are now horizontal, then the lines that appear clearer will have rotated also. This indicates that the distortion is fixed relative to the orientation of the eye rather than being any property of the pattern itself.

Viewing this type of pattern frequently induces reports of pastel colours over the surface, even though none are physically present: the white spaces between the vertical lines might appear pinkish and those between the horizontal greenish or vice versa.[29] One possible basis for these 'subjective colours' concerns another aberration to which the eye is prone: white light passing through the eye is decomposed into its spectral (coloured) constituents, so that different wavelengths of light (colours) are focused in different depth planes.[30] This is called chromatic aberration, a characteristic common to simple lenses, but not to the more sophisticated optical equipment present in modern cameras. Hermann von Helmholtz once said that he would not accept any optical device that had characteristics as poor as the human eye — but he hastened to add that it was remarkable how much is achieved by such a crude optical system.[31] Normally we are not aware of our chromatic aberration, but it could produce the above subjective colours when operating in conjunction with pattern specific astigmatism. In short, if regular astigmatism produces blur in one set of contours, say the verticals, then the chromatic aberration would be enhanced making them appear coloured.[32] The colour in the orthogonal, clearly defined contours is complementary to that produced by the chromatic aberration, as would be expected on the basis of simultaneous colour contrast (see section 1.5). Since the majority of people have some slight regular astigmatism for vertical or horizontal contours these colours would not be expected to occur with patterns having oblique elements, like *1.4.24* — but they should be visible when the pattern is rotated by 45°.

The term 'subjective colours' has been associated almost exclusively with the colours perceived with rotating black and white patterns, but they occur with stationary patterns, too.[33] They might have been noticed in many of the patterns presented earlier in this section. These subjective colours differ from those linked with regular astigmatism: they can occur within patterns comprised of lines having one orientation alone, like figures *1.4.25* and *1.4.26*, and they tend to be in the form of coloured dots moving rapidly over the lines.[34] It is likely that these scintillating coloured dots result from involuntary eye movements over the pattern. As such they seem to be related to the 'streaming' effects that tend to be superimposed on the pattern. Viewing these figures for more than about 30 seconds often results in tiny dots appearing to move back and forth (streaming) perpendicular to the lines. This effect has been called by many names in the past, like snowfall or scintillating currents, and there are also components diagonally to the lines as well as perpendicularly.[35] There is a compelling after-effect associated with prolonged observation, which can be seen either on closing the eyes or looking at a blank surface following 30 seconds or so of observation of the periodic pattern.[36] Again, the after-effect tends to be in terms of dots streaming in a direction perpendicular to the inducing lines.

Both illustrations contain figural elements and variations in spatial frequency: the figures in *1.4.25* are defined by changes in contrast whereas that in *1.4.26* is abstracted from the slight differences in line thickness. The face can be seen more easily when the image is out of focus — either by blurring the image or viewing it from a greater distance. The face can be masked during prolonged observation by the streaming dots described above; thus attempting to extract details of the face by close inspection in turn generates effects that render its visibility more difficult.

The illustrations presented throughout this section represent what is probably the most optical Op Art in that they generally involve some slight optical aberrations of the eye that occur all the time but which are constantly overlooked in our normal perception. Op Artists have made glaringly obvious those processes in perception that go so frequently unnoticed. In these designs they can only be ignored by closing the eyes or looking away, although brief after-effects often accompany such aversion. Indeed, some designs of this kind are so active visually that some people find them disturbing, and even painful, to look at![37]

Op Art

Bridget Riley has been most successful in manipulating these various phenomena, and the scale on which they are executed enhances their dynamism. Her initial paintings were achromatic but more recently she has incorporated colour into the wavy designs that test the limits of our optical resolution.[38]

1.4.1

1.4.3

1.4.4

1.4.5 *Raydons*

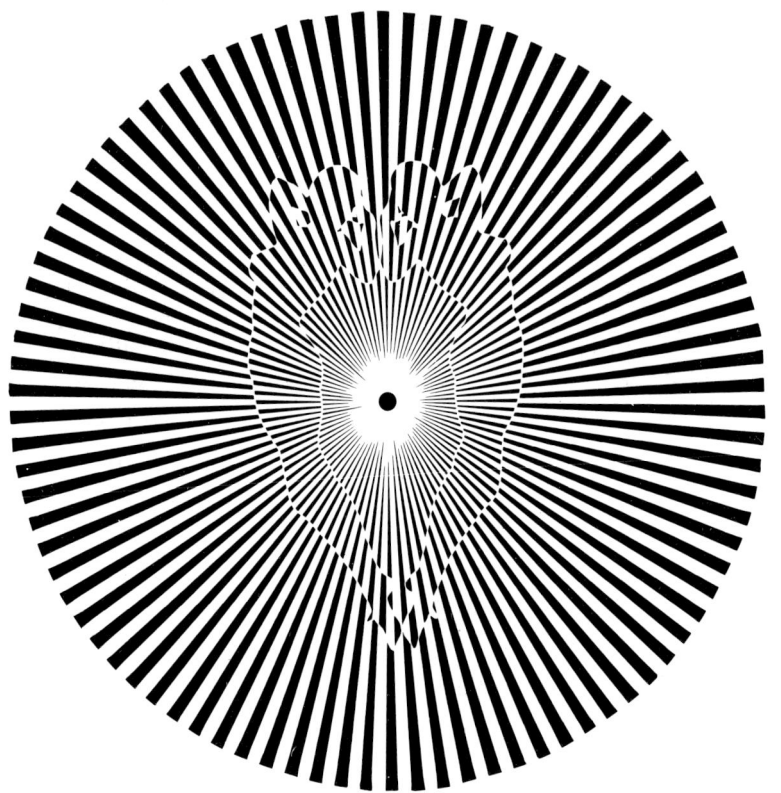

1.4.6

1.4.7 *Chrysanthemum*

1.4.8

1.4.9 *Reflections*

1.4.10

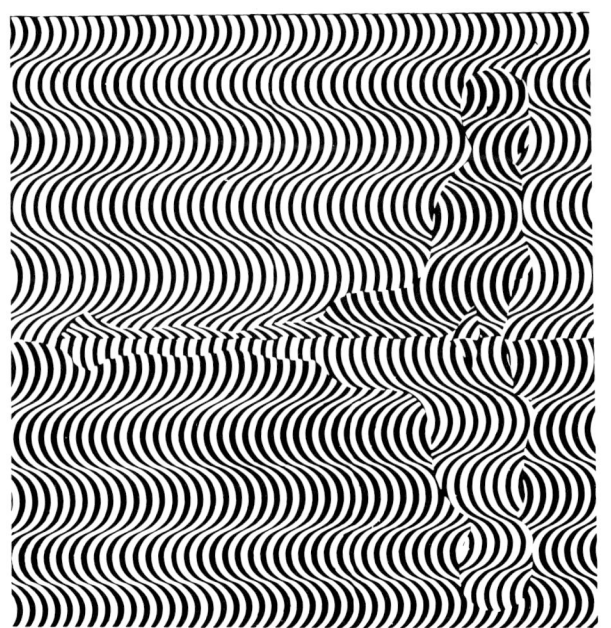

1.4.11

1.4.12

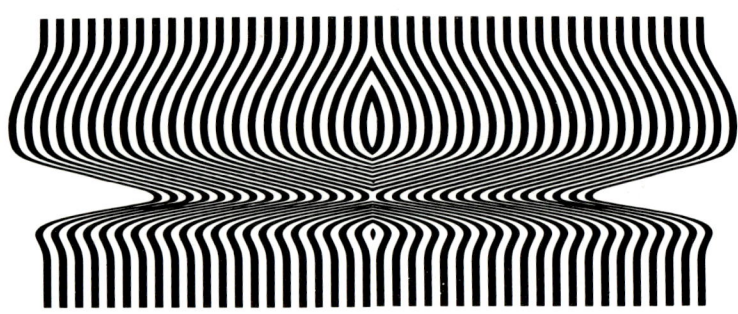

1.4.13

1.4.14 *About Turn*

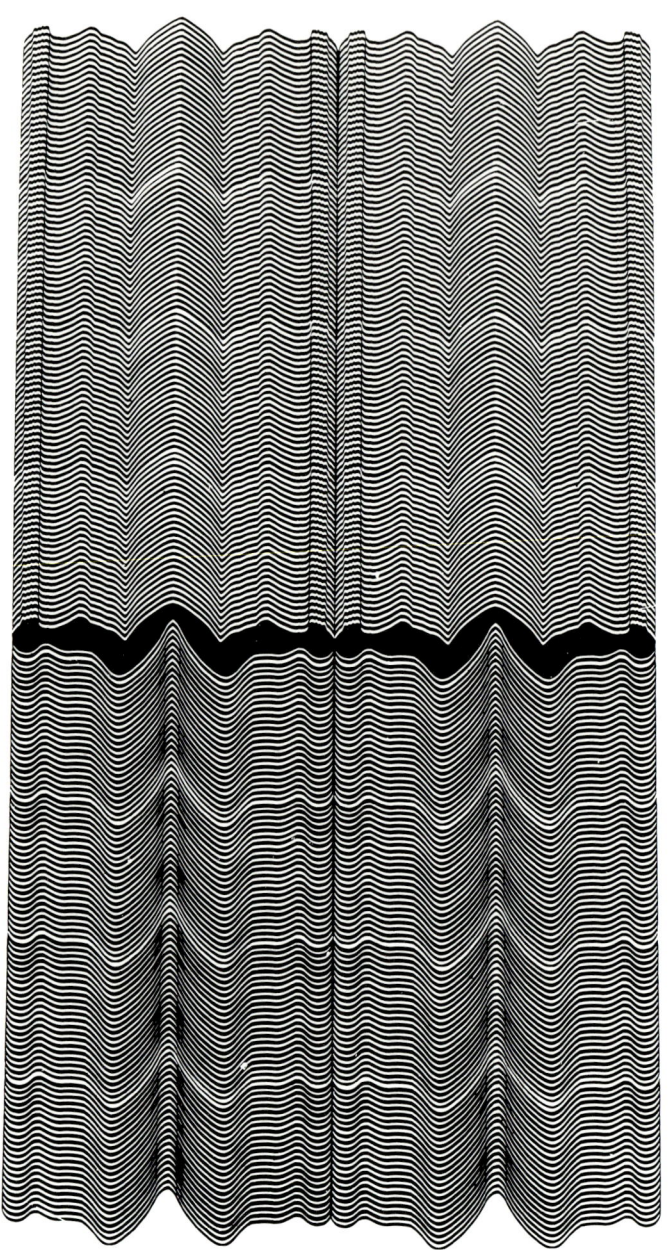

1.4.15 *Curvaceous Border*

1.4.16 *See Nymphs*

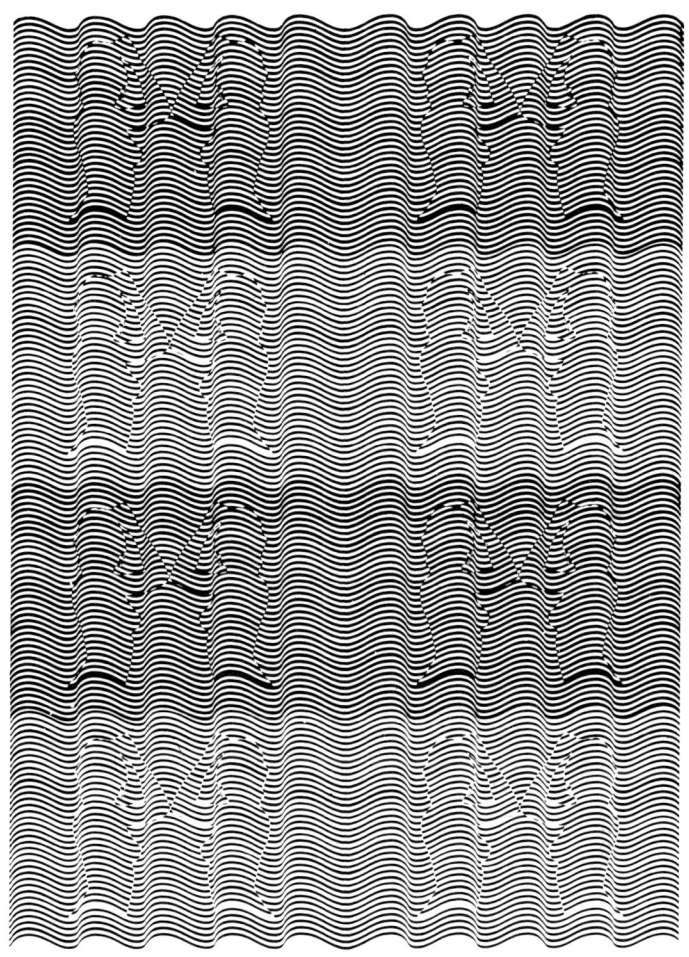

1.4.17 *Bali Dancers*

1.4.18

1.4.19

1.4.20

1.4.21 *The Model*

1.4.22 *Op-position*

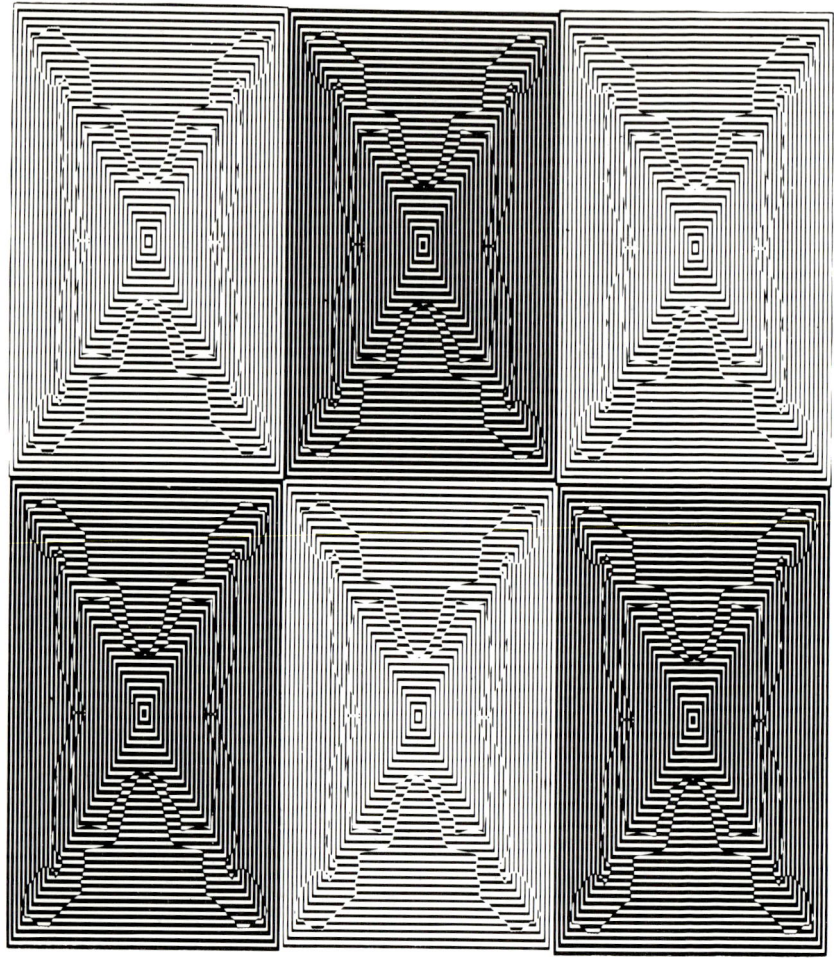

1.4.23

1.4.24

1.4.25 *Spatially Frequent*

1.4.26 *Facial Frequency*

Op Art

1.5 After-images and simultaneous contrast

After-images are familiar occurrences — the patterns seen following stimulation by a very bright light source, like the sun or a photographic flash-gun. In both cases the disc of light is seen after it ceases to be physically present as a stimulus to the eye. The after-image is 'painted on the retina' and it is superimposed in the same position on all objects fixated — it is a stabilized retinal image. The basis for the after-image lies in the bleaching of photochemical pigments in the receptor rods and cones.[39] When the bleaching is so intense that it takes an appreciable period for the photochemicals to be regenerated then an after-image is seen. The bleaching can also derive from prolonged observation of a less intense source. By fixating the centre of *1.5.1* for about a minute and then viewing the adjacent white paper the vase/faces will be seen as an after-image. It might take a little time to develop and it might disappear after several seconds, but it can be reactivated by blinking. It is important to keep the eyes as still as possible initially, otherwise the after-image might not be visible subsequently. The after-image would have appeared whiter than the white paper onto which it was projected, i.e., it has the opposite contrast relations to the real image generating it (called the primary stimulus). In the case of coloured patterns the same procedure will yield an after-image in a colour different to that of the primary stimulus. For example, if *1.5.1* was viewed through, say, a red filter (like a piece of coloured glass or perspex) the vase would still appear black but the background would be red. Following fixation on the pattern a white surface (viewed without the colour filter) will appear as a white vase on a pale greenish background. There is a relatively lawful relationship between the colour of the after-image and that producing it, such that they are complementary. Complementary colours are defined in terms of the mixtures of monochromatic lights (consisting of a narrow band of wavelengths) that yield greyness.[40] Thus, blue and yellow are complementary colours, as are red and green. These after-images generated by black and white or coloured primary stimuli are called negative after-images, but in the case of colour the term complementary is more frequently used. The terms are necessary because after-images can also be positive — having the same contrast or colour as the primary stimulus. Generally a very intense light source is required to produce positive after-images: they are visible before the negative after-image and they last for a shorter period.

After-images occur constantly when viewing high contrast patterns, like those presented in the preceding sections, but they are rarely noticed because the eyes move to fixate on contour-rich areas which can mask the visibility of the after-images. For example, returning to *1.4.9*, the high contrast lines will generate transient after-images that are visible after each movement of the eyes, but they are only apparent when projected onto the white background surrounding the design, and not in the design itself. The 'haloes' that are seen around high contrast edges during fixation are also evidence of after-images: slight instabilities of fixation result in movement of the edges onto retinal areas that have had different amounts of light adaptation. This can be seen in *1.5.2*: during fixation of the small central black dot the black discs will occasionally have white haloes surrounding them, and contrariwise for the white discs. Alternately fixating on the small dots (for about 30 seconds each) will maintain the visibility of the after-images and will complete the triangle always with discs of the same contrast — white on a black background or vice versa. Similar haloes are visible around the ellipses in *1.5.3*. Additionally, the whole pattern tends to be reproduced in negative form following an eye movement — that is, the negative after-images of the black ellipses are projected onto the white background, to appear brighter than the background itself. Since there is insufficient structure within the pattern to maintain fixation within any one area, the eyes move constantly over it. The after-images so produced are brief and disappear rapidly because they result from relatively short periods of fixation. Longer fixation generates more durable after-images. Bridget Riley has used this technique elegantly in paintings of black discs on a white ground.[41]

The occurrence of such after-images provides a simple method for demonstrating the instability of the eyes even when attempts are made to keep them perfectly still. Fixate the central white dot in *1.5.4* for about 30 seconds and then try to keep the eyes directed precisely on the black dot. The negative after-image of the grid will be superimposed, but it will appear to be jumping around, mirroring the involuntary movements of the eyes.[42]

Simultaneous contrast is a phenomenon that has been known to artists for centuries — a colour can have its appearance modified when surrounded by another. As with after-images, simultaneous contrast can operate in both chromatic and achromatic conditions. Examples of achromatic contrast are shown in *1.5.5* and *1.5.6*; each contains two equivalent grey shapes, one flanked by black and the other by white. They do not, however, appear equally bright — those surrounded by black appear lighter than those on white. When grey shapes are embedded in coloured surrounds they no longer look grey, but take on pastel shades complementary to the colour surrounding them. In like manner, colours that look the same when viewed in isolation can appear quite different when placed beside other colours. For example, equivalent green discs on yellow and blue backgrounds will seem bluish-green and yellowish-green, respectively.

The effect of one colour on another surrounded by it does not always yield colour contrast but can, under certain conditions, act in the reverse manner. These are called assimilation effects, and they are most often seen in regular geometrical patterns. For instance, thick red stripes separated by thin yellow stripes appear to have a yellowish tinge, whereas the same red stripes have a darker, slightly bluish, appearance when separated by thin blue stripes. Assimilation effects, like simultaneous contrasts, can be induced in grey as well as coloured fields. Figures eliciting all these phenomena can be found in various books on colour or colour vision.[43]

It is generally considered that simultaneous contrast might be accounted for in terms of neural interactions between neighbouring cells in the visual system. The interactions are of an inhibitory nature so that any differences between the activity of adjacent cells will be enhanced and similarities will be nullified. This is referred to as lateral inhibition, and its operation results in the output of a cell being determined by the relational rather than the absolute levels of stimulation. Lateral inhibition occurs at very early stages within the visual system as well as in the visual cortex, but the relationship between neural inhibition and the phenomena of simultaneous contrast remains problematical.[44]

One further colour phenomenon merits discussion, because it leads to fluctuations in the appearance of enclosed coloured areas. It occurs particularly well with saturated red shapes on a saturated blue background. The boundaries between the red and blue seem to bounce around, often quite suddenly, and when the pattern is moved sideways the red shapes appear to lag behind the blue background. It is somewhat easier to observe under dim illumination. It is generally called the 'fluttering hearts' phenomenon because of the shapes used to demonstrate it in the last century.[45] The basis of the phenomenon remains enigmatic, having been related to differences in the response time of visual receptors to different colours, neural interactions between different colour mechanisms, and the chromatic aberration of the eye.[46]

1.5.1

1.5.2

1.5.3

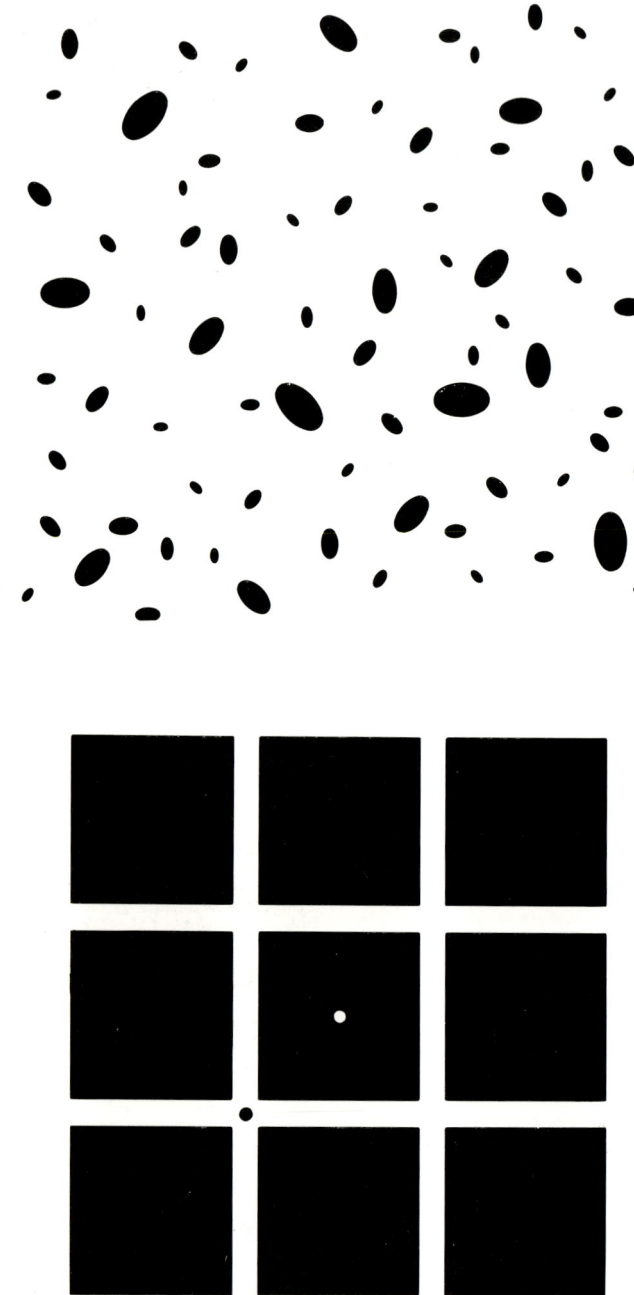

1.5.4

1.5.5

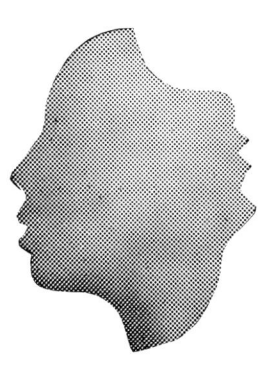
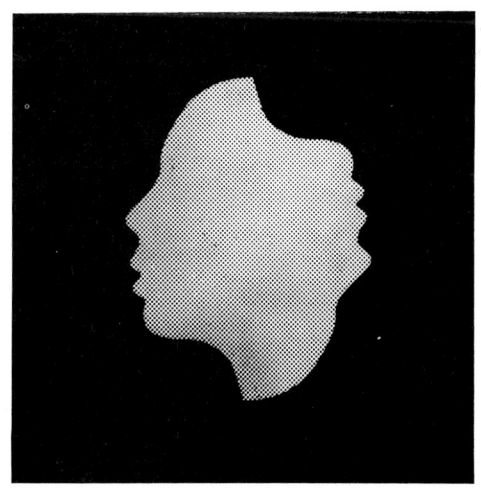

1.5.6

1.6 Grids and checkerboards

Essentially the same processes implicated in simultaneous brightness contrast have been suggested as the basis for the illusory dots seen in *1.6.1*. In the upper half of the figure dark grey dots appear at the intersections of the white lines (other than the intersection fixated), whereas the reverse occurs in the bottom half: light grey dots are visible in the black intersections. The dots do not exist physically on the printed surface, but are a consequence of the way in which the contours and contrasts in the pattern are processed by the brain. The illusion has been known for over a century and it was then considered to be due to simultaneous contrast, although no mechanism was proposed to account for this.[47] More recently, specific hypotheses as to the physiological basis for the so-called Hermann and Hering grid effects have been advanced.[48] The most popular is that the properties of cells in the retina or lateral geniculate body[49] lead to these illusory dots. Neural cells in the visual system respond to particular characteristics of a stimulus falling on a specific part of the retina: the area or pattern that activates the neuron maximally is referred to as the receptive field for that cell. In the retina and lateral geniculate body the neurons respond most strongly to small circular patches of light or dark. If, however, these small circular patches are surrounded by more light or dark, respectively, then the neuron responds less strongly or not at all. In fact, the receptive fields have been found to be concentrically organized, with a circular centre that can be inhibited by its annular surround. Thus, cells with concentrically organized receptive fields will be differentially stimulated by a grid according to the parts of the pattern that stimulates them. Most pertinently, those cells having the centres of their receptive fields falling at an intersection will be inhibited more strongly by their surrounds than will cells with equivalent receptive fields flanked by two square areas. It has been argued that this difference in surround inhibition generates the illusory dots.[50] But this hypothesis seems difficult to sustain in the light of the effects produced by the next two figures (*1.6.2* and *1.6.3*). Both yield conventional Hermann-Hering grids in the top halves; the question is whether any similar effects occur in the outline squares at the bottom. With the outlines alone there would be little difference in the amount of inhibition operating on receptive fields falling at the intersections and on those falling between them. There are certainly some perceptual effects occurring at the outlined intersections — they do not appear to be equivalent to the spaces flanked by the parallel lines. These effects seem to have some similarities with the Hermann-Hering grids, but also some differences. In the lower left quadrants of *1.6.2* and *1.6.3* (with black outlines on a white ground) the dots appear to have a concentric organization with dark centres and surrounds that appear brighter than the white background; the lower right quadrants show the reverse, with small light grey dots surrounded by blacker rings than the background. The dots in the upper quadrants, the Hermann-Hering grids, seem more evenly dispersed within the areas of intersection, and are not surrounded by complementary annuli. In all cases the dots are visible more readily with smooth eye movements over the patterns. Keeping the eyes as still as possible reduces the intensity of the illusory dots, and they might even disappear. If fixation is upon an intersection, no dot is visible there even though they can be seen at the neighbouring intersections. This has been said to reflect the size differences between receptive fields from the central fovea and more peripherally. Varying the dimensions of the intersections, as in *1.6.3*, enables visibility of the dots in and around the area of fixation when the smallest central parts of the quadrants are viewed.

The occurrence of illusory dots in the outline figures casts doubt on the validity of the receptive field hypothesis mentioned above as the sole basis for their visibility.[51] Other processes might also be involved. One such process could be related to the effects visible at the end of lines: *1.6.4* illustrates how gaps in lines lend the impression of contours joining them (see section 1.7). If two such ends are placed orthogonally, as in *1.6.5*, the illusory dots, if they occur at all, are particularly weak.

The limiting dimensions that generate illusory Hermann-Hering dots vary with retinal eccentricity, and this has been used as a method for inferring the size of receptive fields in the human visual system.[52] This is illustrated in *1.6.6* and *1.6.7* — the small dots in the centres of the figures that are visible on close inspection disappear when viewing eccentric parts.

Victor Vasarely has utilized Hermann and Hering grid phenomena in many of his black and white paintings.[53] The surface of the picture plane seems to reverberate with activity, due both to the multitude of illusory dots and to the pattern elements manipulated. In addition to augmenting the vibrancy of the pictures, the dots can be put to illustrative use. That is, their occurrence can be incorporated into the design for pictorial purposes, as in *Snowfall* (*1.6.8*), where they create the impression of snow falling on the tree-like forms. They can also operate to enhance the ambiguity in outline or embedded figures, like

1.6.9 and *1.6.10*.

The dots are illusory in so far as they are not a part of the luminance distribution over the pattern, but when they are generated they can themselves act as elements of yet other configurations. The light grey dots formed at the black intersections of spirals in *1.6.11* are completed, by the phenomenon of good continuation, to form concentric circles. The circles can be seen extending to the circumference occasionally, but are more distinct near the centre. In a sense these form second-order illusions — the illusory circles are made up from dots which are themselves illusory. This technique of generating patterns from the configuration of Hermann or Hering grid dots lends itself to artistic manipulation — although it has not been so used, to the best of my knowledge. Designs *1.6.12* to *1.6.14* present some preliminary examples in which the figure is defined by the good continuation of the illusory dots generated at the intersections. The patterns are designed in a manner similar to that for incorporating figural elements into moiré bands: the location of the dots is manipulated by the variation in line separation which, by completion, induces the curvature.

Checkerboards bear some structural similarities to the grids above, but they offer a different range of phenomena for manipulation. Figure *1.6.15* presents the now familiar, though in this case checkered, faces. They might not be immediately evident as the curved checks create an impression of a folded surface. This folding effect can be seen more readily on the left side of *1.6.16*: the central region of the figure is a regular checkerboard, which is flanked by various compressions of its regularity. Another feature of checkerboards will probably have been noted in this pattern, namely, the appearance of bands connecting the diagonals of the checks. The effect is much easier to see if the patterns are defocused slightly (e.g. by fixating on a point held slightly in front of the page or by squinting) or if they are viewed from the side. In the case of the regular checkerboard the lines are straight and diagonal, but with the outer components they are variously curved.[54] With circular checkerboards (*1.6.17* and *1.6.18*) these curves are themselves spirals in opposite directions and they are modulated according to the separation of the checks. When the checks are themselves formed from oppositely directed spirals then the Fourier components are radial and linear (*1.6.19* and *1.6.20*). These figures display some features similar to those in *1.6.11*, as illusory circles can also be seen surrounding the centre. The effect is more easily seen in *1.6.21*: light circles occur where the black segments meet radially and black circles are visible where they touch laterally. As with the moiré fringes (section 1.3) the light circles are brighter than the surrounding white areas with the converse operating for the black circles. Similar processes of simultaneous contrast, perhaps mediated by lateral inhibitory neural interactions, would seem to be implicated in both cases.

Further variations on the checkerboard theme are displayed in figures *1.6.22* to *1.6.31*, some of which have figures embedded in them, not unlike the examples shown in section 1.2.

1.6.1

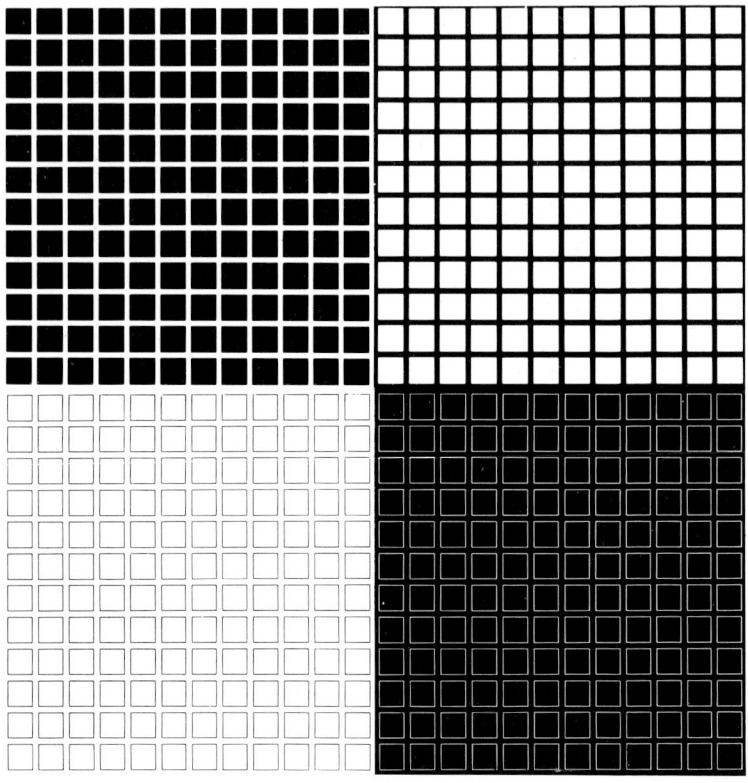

1.6.3

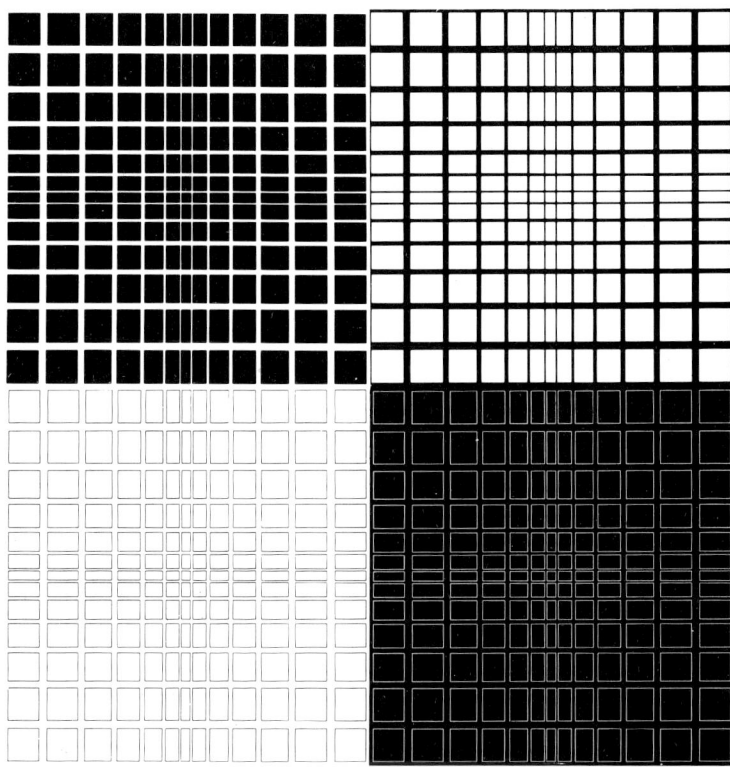

1.6.4

1.6.6

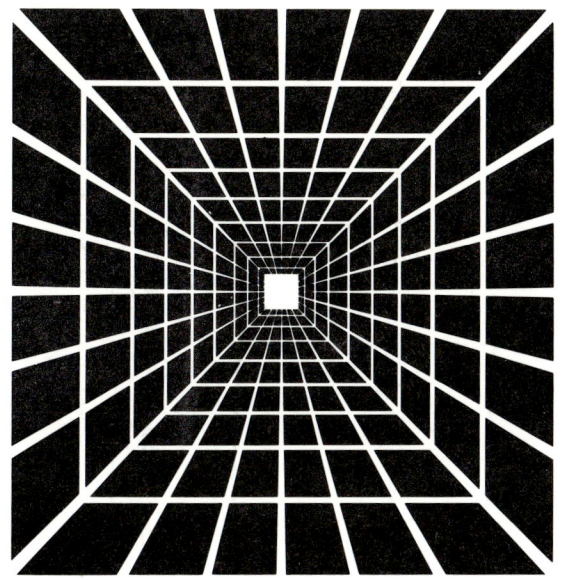

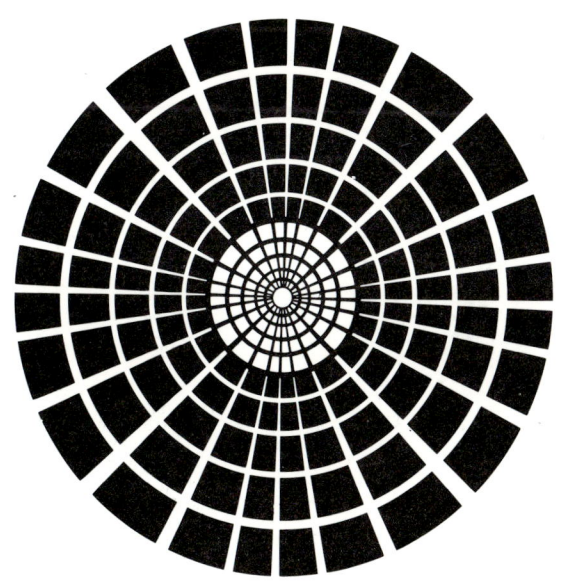

1.6.7

1.6.8 *Snowfall*

1.6.9

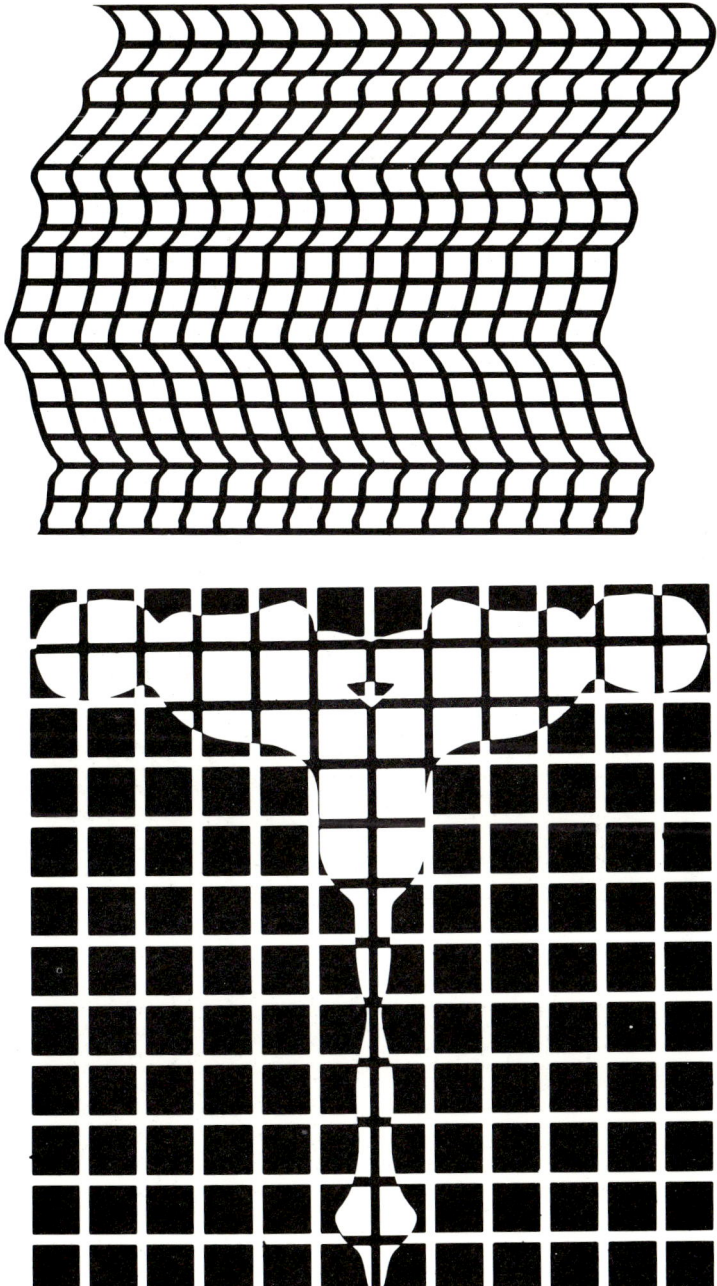

1.6.10

1.6.11

1.6.12

1.6.13

1.6.14

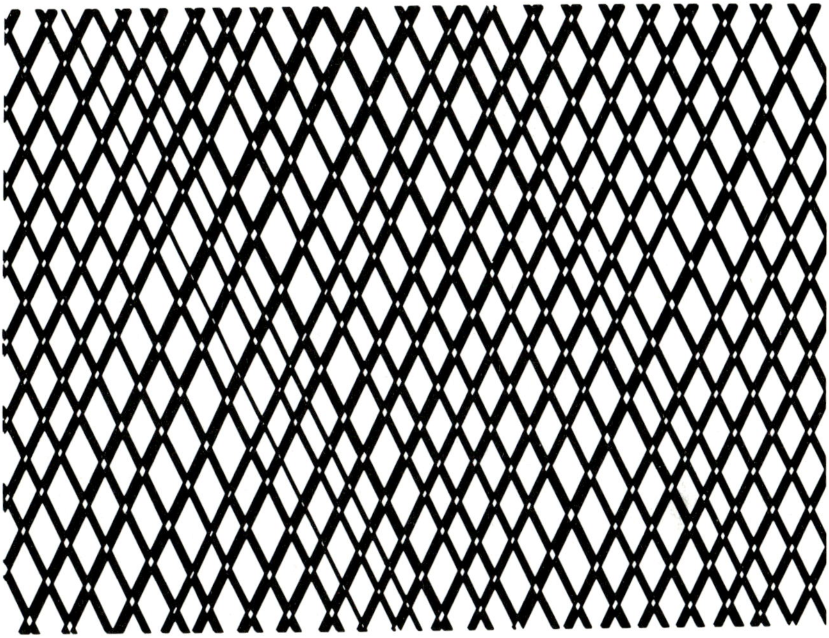

1.6.15

1.6.16

1.6.17

1.6.18

1.6.19

1.6.20

1.6.21

1.6.22

1.6.23

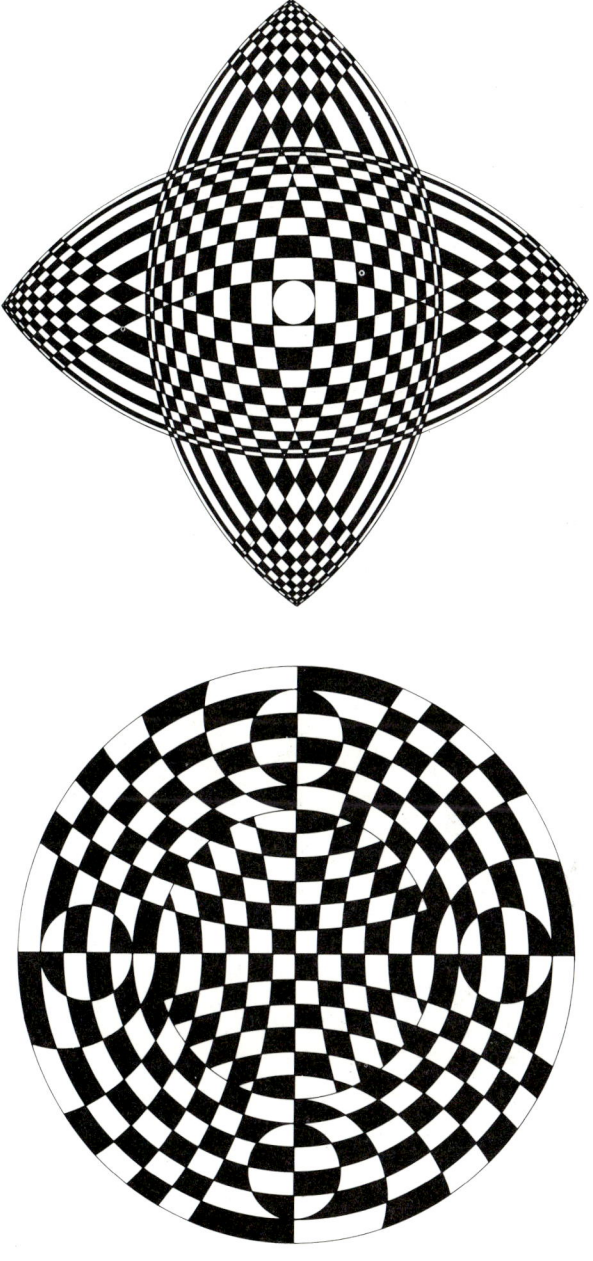

1.6.24

1.6.25

1.6.26

1.6.27

1.6.28

1.6.30

1.6.31

1.7 Subjective contours

A contour is given the physical definition of a luminance boundary, i.e., a change in the amount of light from neighbouring regions. Thus, the letters of this text are physical contours because the amount of light reflected from the white paper is greater than that from the black letters. Such luminance boundaries provide information regarding the objects in the visual environment, and the details within them that allow their recognition. For these reasons the visual analysis of contours has been stressed as of fundamental importance by all contemporary perceptual theorists.[55]

Bearing this in mind, it seems strange that continuous contours are often seen where no physical boundaries in luminance exist. Many examples of such subjective contours can be found in the preceding illustrations, and they can be generated in a number of ways. One method, currently fashionable in psychological research,[56] is shown in *1.7.1*. Circles positioned at the extremities of a figure have some parts missing corresponding to those which would have been occluded by the figure. For simple shapes, like triangles, three circles with missing sectors would suffice to define them (*1.7.2*); in the case of the vase/faces the additional circles are provided to define the edges of the figure. The white area corresponding to the vase probably appears whiter than the white background of the paper, and it seems as though a boundary does exist between the two. However, for large parts of the perceptual boundary that separates the vase from its background there is no physical difference in the luminance. They are called 'subjective contours' in order to stress that their production is within our brains rather than on the picture surface. The subjective contours have not been adequately explained in visual science, but they seem to be closely related to the Gestalt grouping principles described in section 1.2. That is, processes like good continuation are operating to connect the incomplete elements of a figure. Alternative interpretations have stressed that the pattern is judged as one in which an object (the vase) is overlapping and in front of others (the circles).[57] The nearer object would be slightly brighter, hence the subjective contour. It is not at all clear how such a view would handle the alternate appearance of this figure as two profile faces, as these would be nearer than the background. That is the faces should appear brighter at the regions where the subjective contours are generated because they would be perceived as nearer than the background, but it seems that the 'vase' remains brighter even when the faces are visible. The areas defining the faces contain more black regions than that for the vase, and this has led to some more physiologically founded theories for the genesis of the subjective contours.[58] Once more, they have been related to simultaneous contrast effects that would occur within the white sectors of the circles. However, these views do not account for the spreading of the contrast outside the areas of the circles, which is when the subjective contours occur. (The contour can be made to disappear by fixating the region in which it would be produced, as can be seen most clearly in *1.7.2*.) The physiologically based theories also have difficulties in accounting for curvature in the subjective contours, as evident in *1.7.1* and *1.7.3*: the Maltese crosses of the latter contain curved sides, and in the outermost parts these are defined solely by the slight curvature in the segments of the circles. That is, the subjective contours do not simply connect the extremities of the circular segments but retain the continuity given by them.

The circles from which the segments are extracted can themselves be fragmentary (*1.7.4*) and yet the triangles remain visible. Contrariwise, the background can be patterned, as in *1.7.5*, and the subjective triangles appear superimposed upon it. The patterned background in *1.7.5* itself generates an impression of depth — of ambiguous humps and hollows — but these do not seem to influence the line of the subjective edges. The Maltese crosses similarly survive fragmentation of the constituent circles and striation of the background (*1.7.6* and *1.7.7*). Indeed, the subjective triangles remain visible with simultaneous fragmentation of the circles, so that they themselves are formed by completion, and patterning of the background (*1.7.8*).

In the last figure the circles were defined by the endings of lines alone, and this provides another means for generating subjective contours. For example, the Rubin figure can be seen in *1.7.9* even though it is only the termination of lines that provide the elements requiring completion for it. The subjective boundary cannot be associated with any differences in average luminance in this case, since this is virtually the same throughout the pattern. It was noted in the previous section that certain brightness enhancement occurs at the ends of lines (see *1.6.4*). If this was the sole factor involved in seeing the figure in *1.7.9* then the subjective contour might be expected to snake around the ends of the lines, whereas the contours appear to be continuous. Moreover, all the lines are horizontal, so that the astigmatic effects mentioned above should not be operating to render some parts of the pattern blurred relative to others. The heads in *1.7.10* are similarly defined by line discontinuities. Figure *1.7.11* looks much the same at

Op Art

first glance, but closer inspection will reveal heads directed rightwards: these latter are specified by slight changes in line thickness. Actually, close inspection is not the most appropriate way of seeing the faint heads since they are visible more readily with slightly blurred images.

A further, related technique for producing subjective contours involves removing parts of a figure, as in *1.7.12*. Here the letters of the word are broken at invervals, but the breaks are interpreted as a curved ribbon or some such lying over the letters.[59] Clearly the completion effects involved here are similar to those for the triangles above, and further examples are given in *1.7.13* to *1.7.15*. In the case of *Rückstrahlung* (*1.7.15*) there is considerable shimmer due to the curved background lines: these, in fact, reflect the same contours as the back of the figure formed by the breaks in them.

One of the most commonly occurring instances of subjective contours derives from shadow effects. Again these can be illustrated by Rubin's figure (*1.7.16*), but they are perhaps most effective with letters (*1.7.17* to *1.7.19*). The words appear to have a completeness and a sense of solidity due to the shadowing, even though no letter is entirely outlined. By varying the length (*1.7.18*) or the shape of the shadows (*1.7.19*) the surfaces upon which the 'solid' letters appear to be projected seem to be tilted or wavy.

Yet another means of inducing subjective contours is by varying the points at which lines change in orientation. Examples of this type have already been incorporated into some designs (e.g. *1.3.7*, *1.3.34*, *1.3.38*), and in *1.7.20* they dimly define a head. The changing orientation of the lines also gives the impression of the head in relief — as though a striped cloth had been draped over a raised head. Four faces or profiles are so depicted in *1.7.21*. The orientation changes in *1.7.22* lie along curved lines, and give the appearance of either a goblet or a receding tunnel with cambered sides. In the remaining designs (*1.7.23* to *1.7.26*) the completion along the points of orientation all signify figural elements, some of which are easier to recognize than others.

It is evident that subjective contours can be generated in a variety of ways — not only those described in this section but also the completion effects of illusory dots illustrated in section 1.6. It is unlikely that all will eventually be accounted for by a single mechanism, although one feature is common to all configurations giving rise to subjective contours, namely the incorporation of incomplete fragments of figures. These fragments, be they sectors of circles, line endings, illusory dots or shadows, are completed to give the impression of an edge where no physical boundary exists. Hence, whatever mechanism is at the seat of

135

Op Art

Gestalt completion or good continuation is likely to be involved in subjective contours, too.

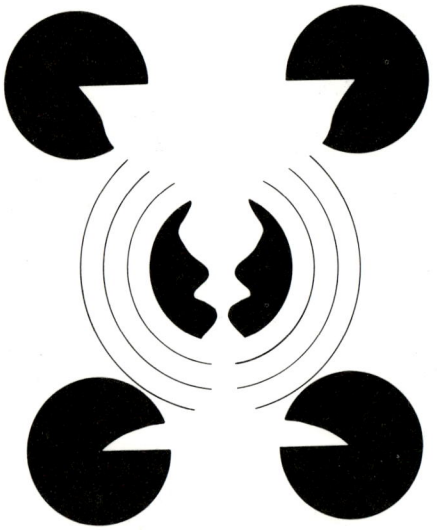

1.7.2

1.7.3

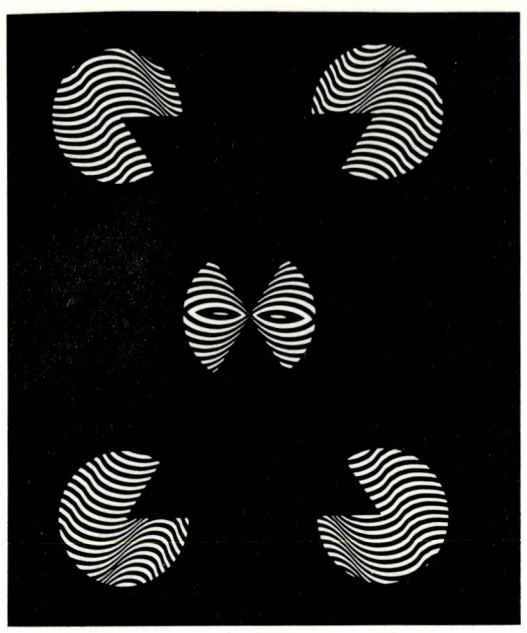

1.7.4

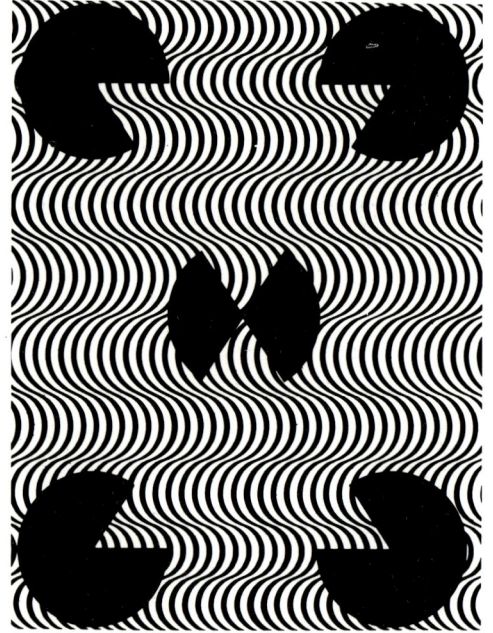

1.7.5

1.7.6

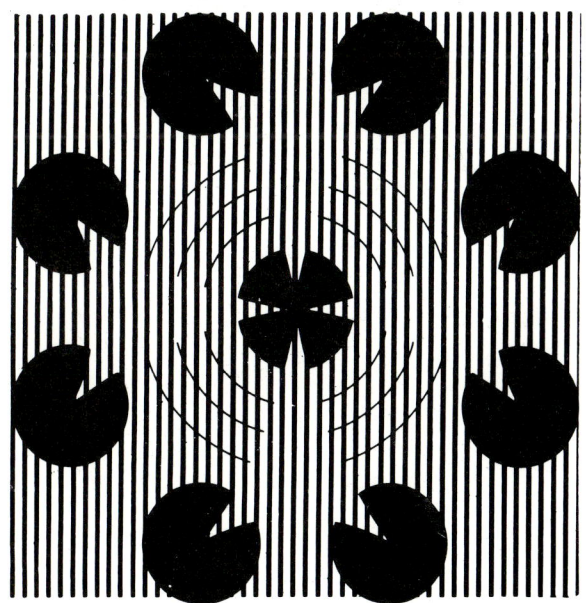

1.7.7

1.7.8

140

1.7.9

1.7.10

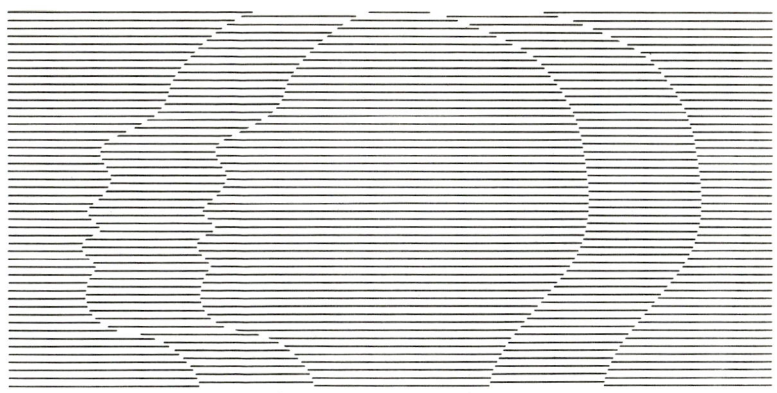

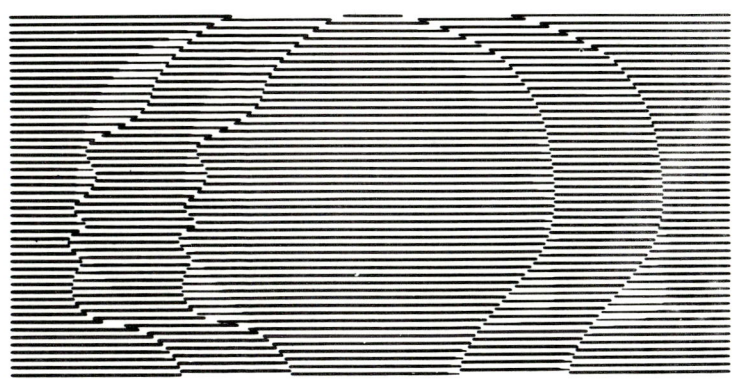

1.7.11

1.7.12

1.7.13

1.7.14

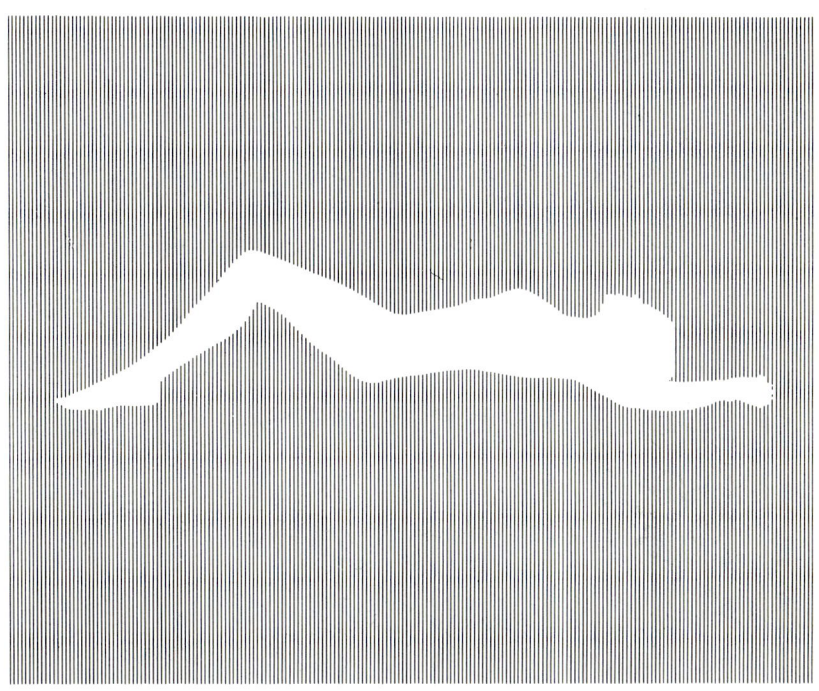

1.7.15 *Rückstrahlung*

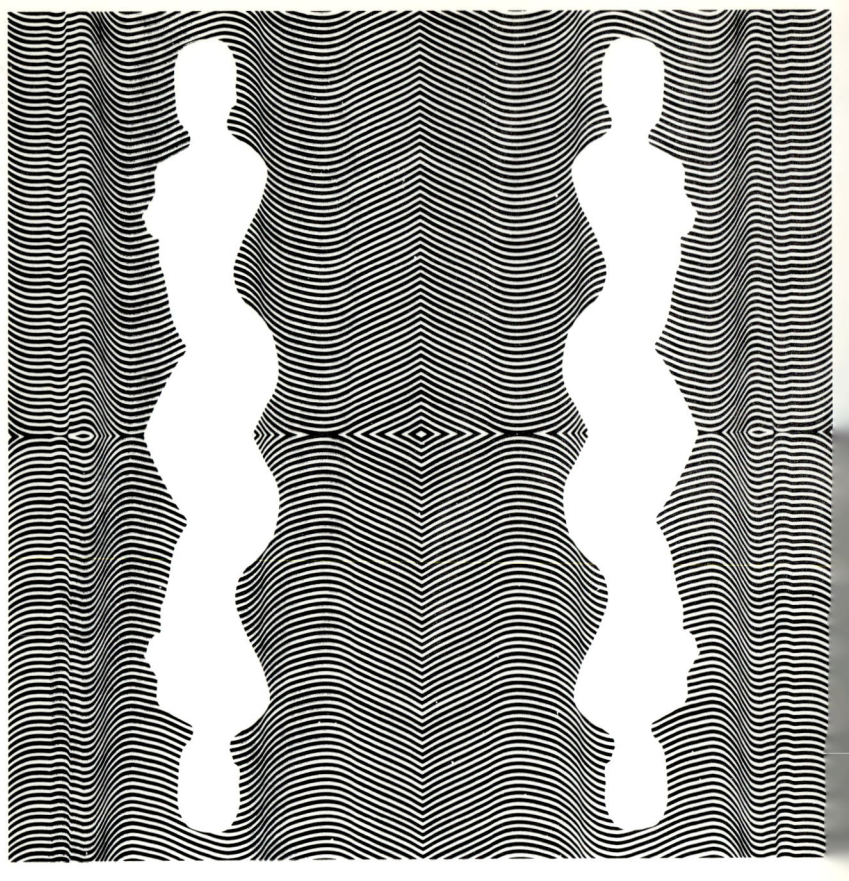

1.7.16

1.7.17

OP-TRICKS

TILT

1.7.18

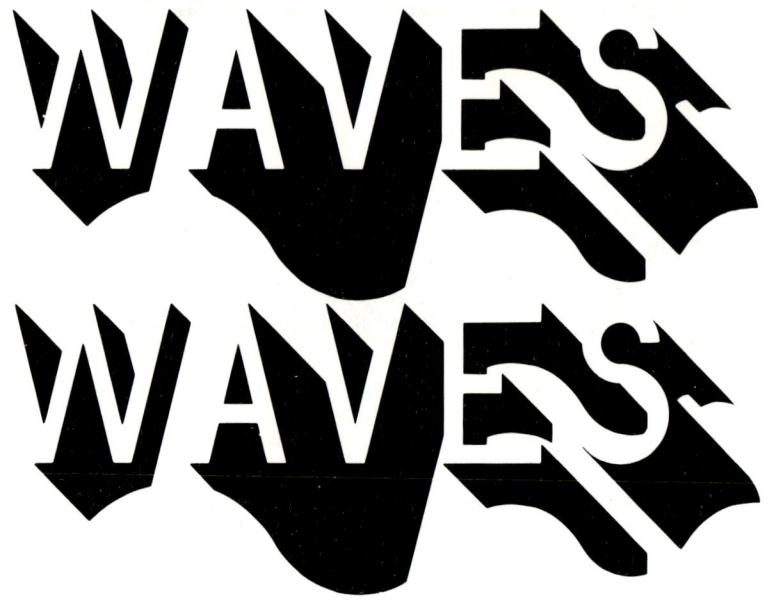

1.7.21

1.7.22

1.7.23

1.7.24

1.7.25 *Topol*

1.7.26 *Outward Facing*

Op Art

1.8 Binocular rivalry

Almost all the phenomena illustrated thus far can be observed by a single eye. Normal vision is, of course, binocular. The two paradoxical features of binocular vision concern the differences in the images projected to each eye: on the one hand, these are ignored to provide singleness of vision, and on the other hand, the disparities are utilized to give stereoscopic depth perception. That is, the world is seen singly despite the two views of it, but it is seen in depth because of these two views. This paradox has puzzled students of vision for 150 years, since the stereoscope was invented.[60] Two processes have typically been adumbrated to account for binocular singleness and depth — fusion and suppression.[61] Unfortunately, these have been considered to be mutually exclusive processes and, since both can be given phenomenal support, the theoretical debate has ossified. There is no reason why both processes could not be in operation, with fusion mediating singleness and stereopsis for small disparities and suppression maintaining singleness for large disparities.

Suppression between the eyes can be demonstrated by the phenomenon of binocular rivalry, which is produced by differences in the colour and/or form of the images presented to each eye. This can be observed most easily using a stereoscope, but there are other methods for separating the images presented to each eye. One such method is to direct the eyes so that they converge either beyond or before the plane of the paper in order to bring one of the adjacent displays into the optical axis of each eye. Most people find this technique difficult to employ because the normal close association between accommodation and convergence needs to be disrupted. The method suggested for use here requires a simple plane mirror, preferably rectangular in shape though most reasonably sized mirrors will suffice. The mirror should be placed with its upper side aligned with the nose and the centre of the forehead and its base directed between the two patterns. If the reflecting surface is towards the right side then the reflected image will undergo a left-right reversal with respect to the printed pattern, and it will also appear slightly smaller than the left pattern (provided the printed dimensions of the two are the same). The direction from which the reflected image appears to come can be changed by moving the bottom of the mirror to the left or right. It is possible to view the left pattern directly with the left eye and the right, reflected, image can be adjusted to be in the same visual direction. That is, the two patterns appear to occupy the same positions in space. If the reflected image was

151

the same as the non-reflected image, then a single pattern would be perceived. However, in all the examples presented the left and right patterns differ (when reflected in the mirror), and this results in binocular rivalry.

Binocular rivalry refers to the alternation in visibility of the patterns, as can be seen when *1.8.1* is viewed using the mirror technique described. It will be noted that the rivalry is not necessarily of a whole monocular field, but often mosaics made up from parts of each pattern are visible. This signifies that the suppression does not operate only between the global patterns for each eye but also for local areas within the monocular fields. Frequently, one of the alternatives is visible for longer than the other, which could signify differences in the intensity of illumination of the patterns. However, even when the two patterns are equated for luminance and any other pattern characteristics that can influence rivalry, one of the alternatives may still be visible for longer. This reflects the dominance of one eye over the other in terms of its suppressive power.[62]

The component lines of *1.8.1* are perpendicular to one another when combined binocularly, and this leads to marked changes in the visibility of the patterns over time. It is, however, not essential for the lines to be perpendicular for rivalry to occur. The component curves in *1.8.2* vary from virtual coincidence in the centre towards orthogonality at the upper and lower flanks, but the rivalry continues in a similar manner. The density of the contours in the component patterns themselves influence the course of rivalry, and it has been suggested that the strength of suppression can be related to this. Thus, the diamond pattern in *1.8.3* might be expected to suppress the concentrically curved pattern for longer than it is suppressed by it, and the different densities within the components of *1.8.4* might show local suppression variations. For simple patterns in which the lines are almost the same orientation they will be seen singly without alternation. However, if the line spacing (spatial frequency) varies for the same orientation they will undergo rivalry, as in *1.8.5*.

To the best of my knowledge, binocular rivalry has not been manipulated systematically by Op Artists, despite its many attractions. One of the common methods for presenting different images to the eyes uses complementary coloured filters before the eyes and superimposed patterns printed in the same colours. These are called anaglyphs (see note 60). The filters are usually red and green, and they have been used in the cinema to make the scenes appear to be three-dimensional. The filters result in the complementary coloured image being seen as

Op Art

black against the background of the filter colour, and so two different black images can be produced.

Anaglyphs have been employed mostly to present stereoscopic images to the eyes and this has proved most successful with patterns composed of randomly spaced dots having some parts displaced in the two monocular fields.[63] The displaced parts stand out in depth relative to the background. This technique does not lend itself readily to blending with the other phenomena described above. However, as was mentioned briefly in section 1.3, depth effects can be generated with transparencies. When they are held some distance from the underlying pattern the relative positions of the moiré fringes differ in each eye. These differences can result in rivalry or stereopsis, depending upon their magnitude. The attraction of random-dot stereograms to visual scientists has been the absence of any monocular cues to depth present in the component stereopairs; the same advantage is shared by moiré-induced stereopairs.

If certain rivalrous patterns are presented as anaglyphs they can also interact to produce moiré fringes. These are in the colour corresponding to the mixture of the two used for printing and are visible without the filters. That is, the designs work at two levels — the monocular (without filters) and the binocular (with them), and so the interactions between the components can combine in the former and compete in the latter. The moiré interactions are lost when the patterns are viewed through coloured filters, because they pass only one colour component to each eye. Figures *1.8.6* to *1.8.10* would generate intricate moiré fringes when superimposed, but will yield marked rivalry when viewed with a mirror, in the manner described above.

When the lines in the component monocular fields are perpendicular then rivalry is easy to observe, as in *1.8.11* to *1.8.13*. In each design there are discontinuities in the parallel lines: for *1.8.11* they generate subjective contours that are circular, and these may influence the regions over which suppression operates. For *1.8.12* and *1.8.13* the embedded patterns are themselves ambiguous, being the familiar vase/faces in *1.8.12* and a horse/human form in *1.8.13*. Superimposing patterns of orthogonal contours that are in complementary colours can lead to perceptual instability even when they are viewed without any filters. For example, if the two pairs in *1.8.11* to *1.8.13* were printed in red and green and superimposed they would appear to vary in visibility. The patterns need to be viewed for some time, during which the horizontal and vertical lines fluctuate in clarity. This has been called monocular rivalry or pattern alternation.[64] It is not as pronounced as

Op Art

binocular rivalry in so far as one set of lines rarely disappears completely; rather their clarity fluctuates so that sometimes the verticals are very indistinct and at other times the horizontals. The monocular rivalry occurs most strongly when the colours are complementary, and it appears to be an ideal candidate for inclusion in the armoury of the perceptually inclined artist.

Op Art is directly concerned with generating some visual tension by the arrangement and interaction of high contrast linear elements. The visual tensions are multiplied in these works which tap processes of binocular competition which generate their own dynamics.

1.8.1

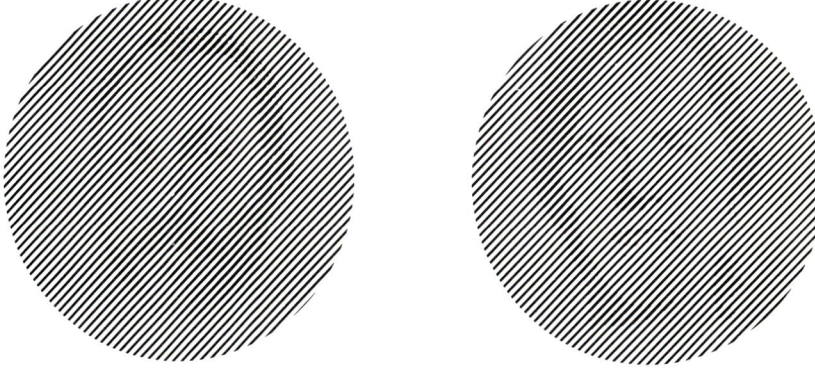

1.8.2

1.8.3

1.8.4

1.8.5

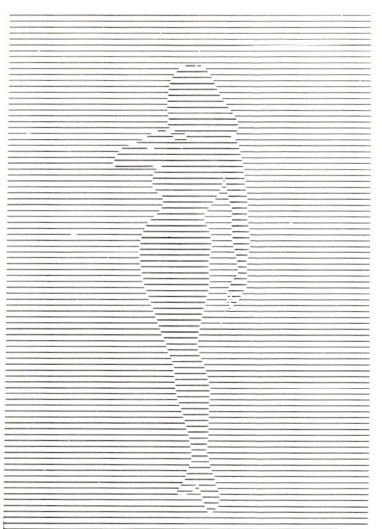 

1.8.6

1.8.7

1.8.8

1.8.9

1.8.10

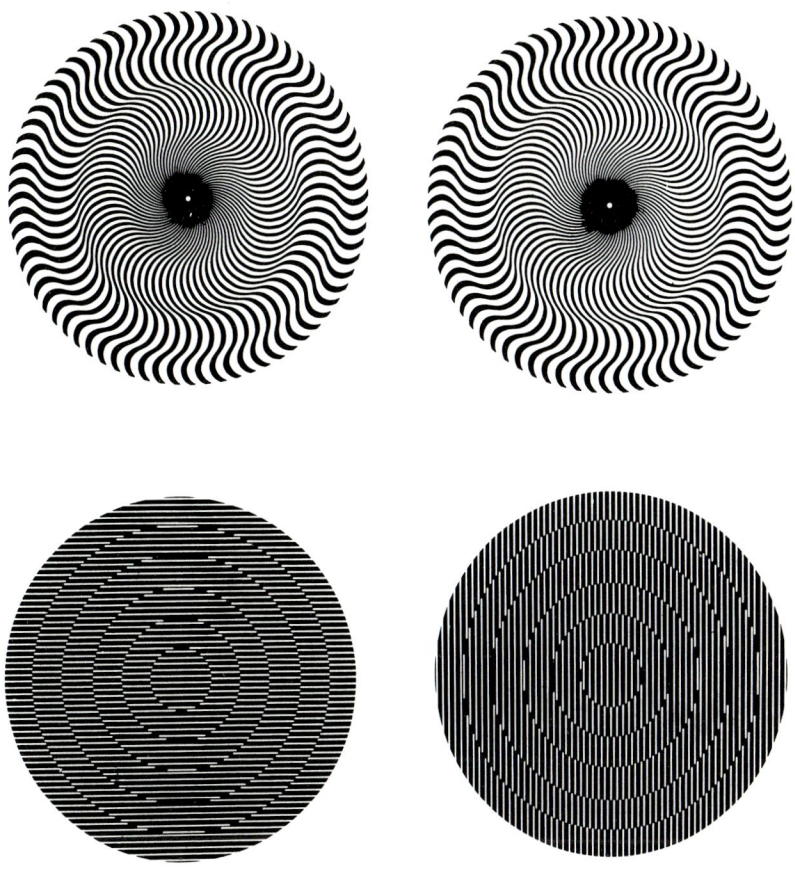

1.8.11

1.8.12

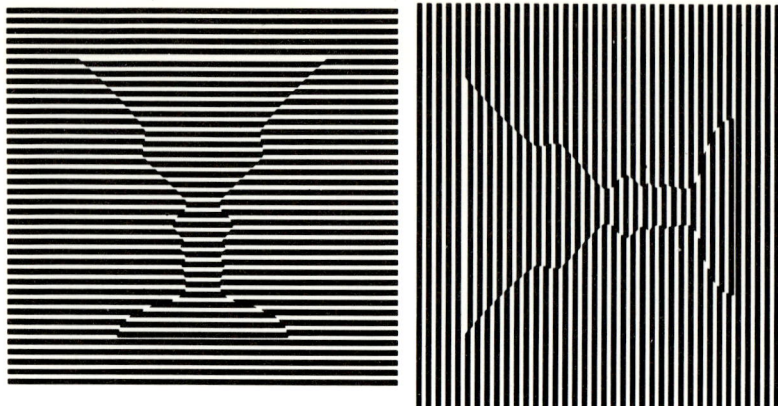

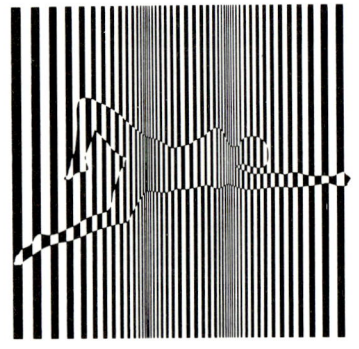

1.8.13

Op Art

1.9 Summary

The phenomena described in the sections above are some of those incorporated into Op Art works. Many other phenomena will be involved but it is considered that these might be the principal ones. Certainly the pattern elements modulated in Op Art are the ones that would be used to elicit the phenomena. Since something is known about the visual processes underlying these phenomena it could be argued that the visual art has been reduced to visual science. Such an argument would be erroneous because it equates understanding the bases of phenomena with the uses to which they are put. Understanding the rules of perspective does not reduce the appreciation of their artistic implementation. Similarly, the interpretation of phenomena at one level need not diminish the fascination with their expression at another level.

The phenomena discussed have a long history in visual science and yet the best examples of their operation can be found in Op Art. This does not reflect very favourably on the ability of visual scientists to represent the subject matter of their own inquiry. In many cases preoccupation with a visual effect for over a century has failed to provide an illustration of it that would not pale into insignificance by the side of examples taken from a decade of Op Art. The reason for this lies not with visual science specifically but with science in general. The all embracing notion of science is simplicity, both in experimentation and interpretation. The visual scientist has followed this principle by simplifying the phenomena under study or, more correctly, representing them visually in their simplest form. The artist has not felt so constrained.

Nowhere has this search for simplicity been more evident than in the study of the geometrical optical illusions. Countless attempts have been made to reduce them to their fundamental form and yet we remain ignorant as to their bases. As stated at the outset, the concern of this book is to explore movements in the opposite direction to simplicity. That is, to complicate matters intentionally; to produce configurations that confound as many phenomena as possible – particularly those mentioned above and the classical geometrical illusion distortions. Before embarking on this course it is necessary to introduce the area of geometrical illusions, which is the topic of the next chapter.

2 Geometrical illusions

2.1 Introduction

'Visual illusions reveal visual truths' stated Jan Evangellista Purkinje, one of the most astute observers in the history of visual science.[1] Whether such confidence would be voiced some 160 years later seems doubtful. The belief that illusions hold the key to unlock the mysteries of vision has been maintained in the face of mounting evidence to the contrary. The alternative, and to my mind more defensible, reason for studying illusions is their inherent fascination.

Geometrical illusions are relatively small distortions of visual space. The distortions can relate to size, shape, direction or movement. They are called illusions because the configurations all contain the potential information that could lead to correct spatial perception, but this does not occur. Rather, systematic errors are made that can be shown to be due to the presence of specific distorting elements. This class of illusions is that labelled geometrical optical by Oppel in 1855.[2] Some twenty years earlier a different type of illusion was reported by a Swiss crystallographer called Necker.[3] He drew attention to the perceptual fluctuations that occurred when observing drawings of simple three-dimensional structures — they show perspective reversals. Many flat outline drawings have this tendency to be perceived in ambiguous depth. The depth is ambiguous in so far as insufficient information is provided for stable perception. These are treated together with another class of figures that provide conflicting depth information over their surface such they could not be constructed in three dimensions — hence the label 'impossible figures'. Reversing and impossible figures will be presented following illustration and discussion of the geometrical optical illusions.

Geometrical illusions

The study of geometrical optical illusions would be assisted greatly by the existence of an unambiguous taxonomy — some grouping that would, hopefully, assist in any general explanation of their basis. Unfortunately, no system of classification has emerged that is not fraught with exceptions,[4] with the consequent uncertainty regarding the scope encompassed by the various theoretical approaches. The illusions need to be demonstrated prior to examining their interpretations, which is the purpose of the next section.

2.2 Geometrical optical illusions

The old-fashioned term for geometrical illusions is used above in order to distinguish the following illusions from the broader category which incorporates figure ambiguity and impossibility. The specific illusions have generally been named after those individuals who first reported their occurrence. The listing given below draws heavily on the excellent text by Robinson.[5]

Many illusions can be demonstrated by the simple expedient of superimposing a transparency of fragments of the configuration over the remaining parts. First place transparency *2.2** over a white surface. It is hoped that the two lines appear straight, equal in length, parallel and with their ends aligned and that the two enclosed shapes are equal in size, circular and with their centres aligned. Placing the transparency over figures *2.2.1* to *2.2.11* and registering them will modify the appearance of all these dimensions. The advantage of this demonstrational technique is that the writer does not have to refer continually to either the trust or the ruler of the reader. Inverting the transparency, so that the circles are uppermost, will yield another set of illusions, most of which are variants of those named. Moreover, when the transparency is moved over the underlay the variations in the distortions can be observed. This works particularly well for the orientation distortions (*2.2.5* to *2.2.10*).

Not all classical illusions are demonstrated here, as they do not all lend themselves to this mode of display. For example, the vertical-horizontal illusion is shown in its various guises in *2.2.12* to *2.2.15*. The basic illusion is that vertical and horizontal extents that are equal physically do not appear so — the vertical looks longer. This illusion is enhanced by bisecting the horizontal line with the vertical rather

---

* The transparent overlay patterns can be found in the envelope inside the back cover. Transparency *2.2* can be used with figures *2.2.1* to *2.2.11*.

163

Geometrical illusions

than them meeting at their ends (*2.2.12*). The variations in illusion magnitude with the orientation of their parts can be seen in *2.2.13* and *2.2.14*. The illusion operates with completed squares, and when a square is rotated by 45° the vertical diagonal looks longer than the horizontal (*2.2.12*). A square can be defined by lines in different orientations, which can modify the apparent rectangularity of the figures (*2.2.15*).[6]

Misperception of curvature is shown in *2.2.16* and *2.2.17*. In all cases the arcs drawn are of circles having the same diameter, although the apparent curvature decreases with the reduction in the extent of the arc. This in turn can lead to a misperception of equal areas bounded by arcs[7] (*2.2.17*).

The apparent orientation of lines can be influenced by a slightly tilted surround. This tilt illusion[8] is shown in *2.2.18*. All the lines in the small circles are vertical, but those in the middle and bottom figures look tilted clockwise, due to the counter-clockwise tilt of the surrounding lines. In the lowest figure the clockwise outer lines will change the apparent orientation of the intermediate ones. Does this change the magnitude of the illusion operating on the central vertical lines?

Perceptual errors of both size and orientation occur in certain figures having light and dark areas. The two squares in *2.2.19* are equal in size, but the white one appears larger. Helmholtz called this an irradiation illusion, as the white square seems to bore into the black surround and the white surround into the black square.[9] A similar effect can be noted in *2.2.20*, although here it is associated with an illusion of orientation: the horizontal lines seem to splay out in different directions.[10] Here the irradiation is operating asymmetrically so that only one end of the white rectangles is surrounded by black ones. These illusions are also related to the direction distortions illustrated most effectively by Fraser at the beginning of the century.[11]

Figures *2.2.21* and *2.2.22* show the spiral and line types of illusion: symmetrical elements in a pattern (the intersections of the radiating spirals or the aligned squares) are connected asymmetrically. The local asymmetrical elements are prepotent perceptually. Thus, in the spiral version (*2.2.21*) all the local spiral elements (due to the asymmetrical connections) occur along the circumference of a circle. The observer is usually entreated to evince surprise at this fact. However, the circular element is a global abstraction whereas the spiral elements are physically present. The same approach applies to the aligned squares in *2.2.22*. The puzzle is that these figures have intrigued psychologists for so long when the perception is veridical with respect to the local features in the patterns. Perhaps one reason for the preoccupation with Fraser's patterns is that they are structurally more complex than the run-of-the-mill illusion figures presented above. Unlike examples of the latter, few psychologists have produced their own Fraser spirals, even though Fraser himself gave reasonably precise directions for their construction.[12]

This concludes the demonstration of most classical geometrical optical illusions. A little will now be said of their possible bases.

2.2.1 (a) *Müller-Lyer*

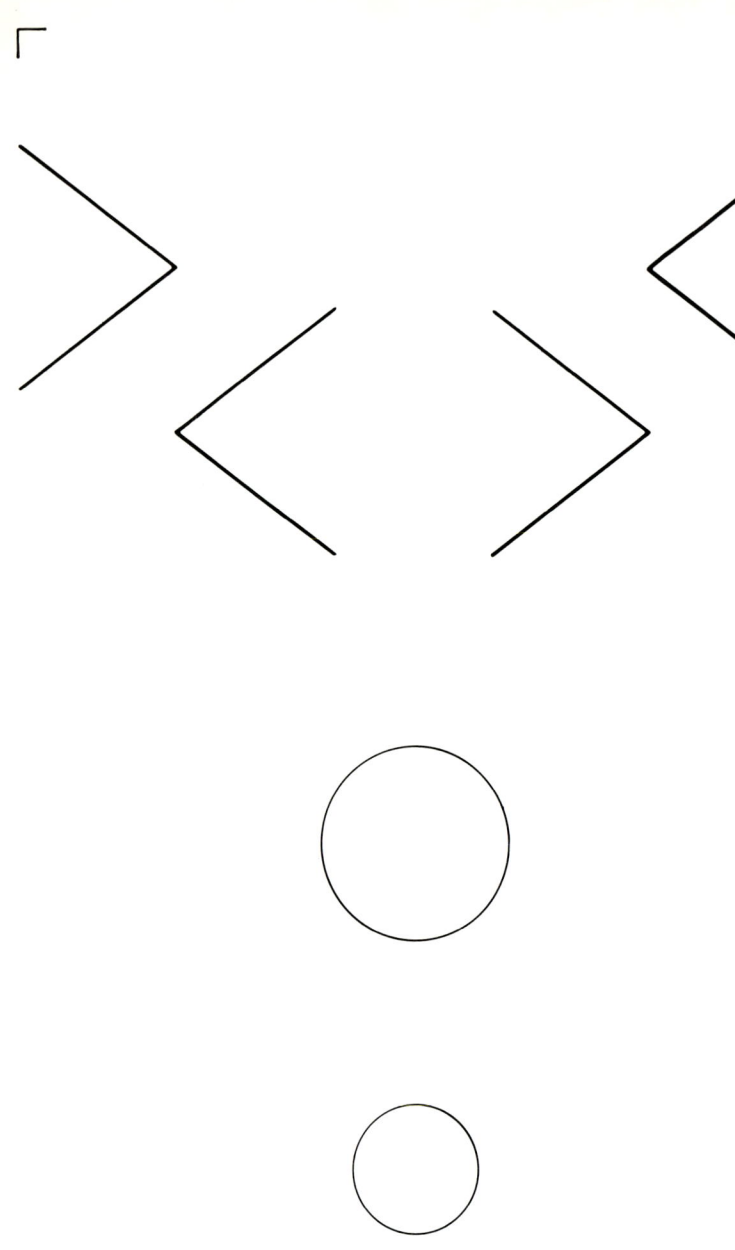

(b) *Delboeuf*

2.2.2 (a) *Ponzo*

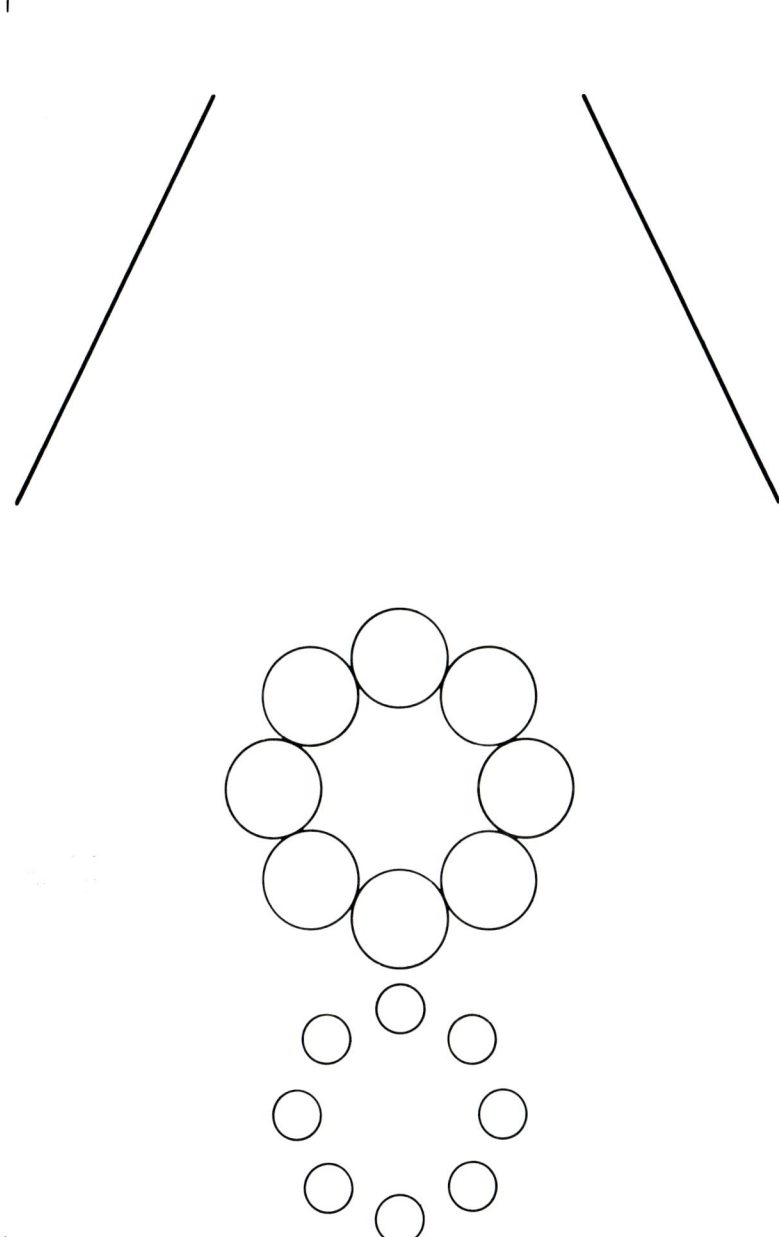

(b) *Titchener*

2.2.3 (a) *Poggendorff*

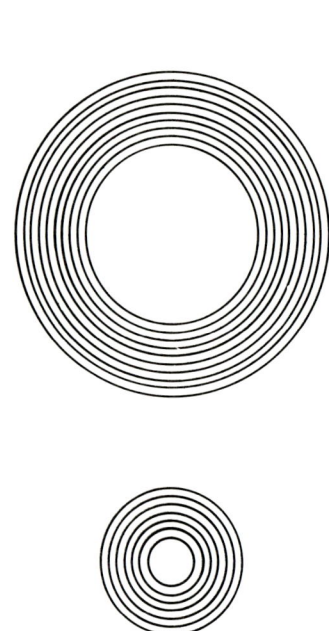

(b) *Tolansky Variant*

2.2.4 (a) *Oppel-Kundt*

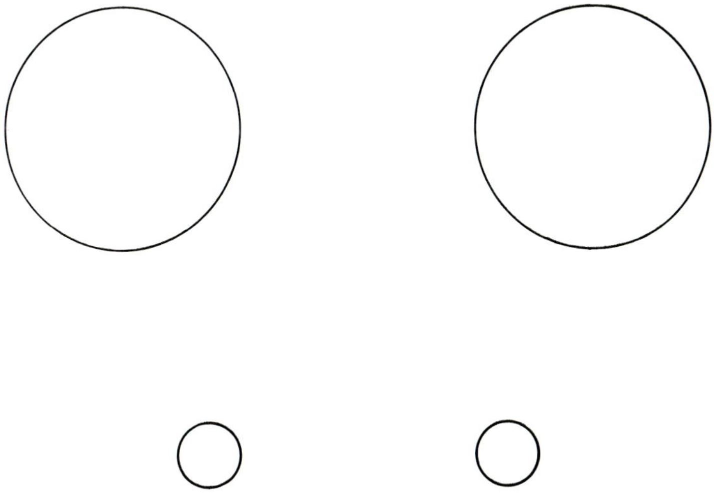

(b) *Lipps*

169

2.2.5 (a) *Zöllner*

(b) *Orbison*

2.2.6 (a) *Zöllner Variant*

(b) *Luckiesh*

2.2.7 (a) *Wundt*

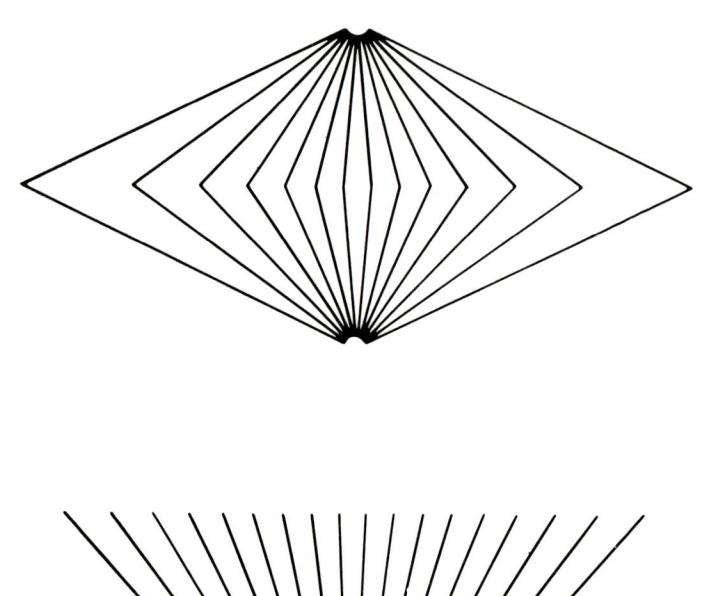

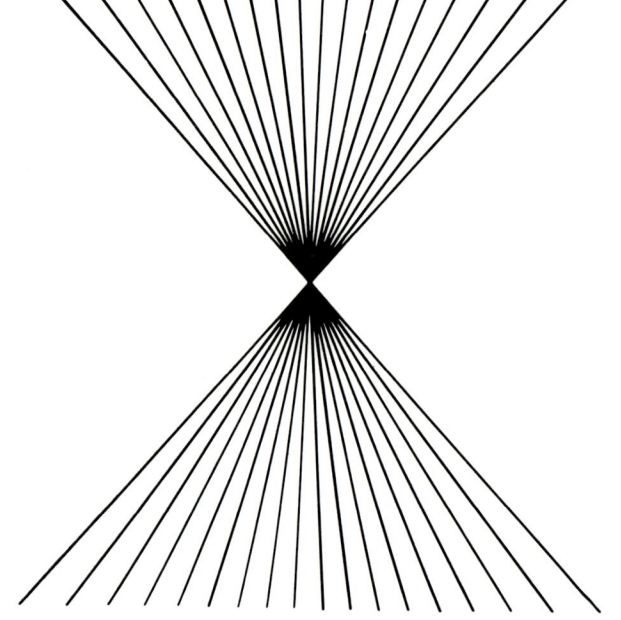

(b) *Ehrenstein*

2.2.8 (a) *Oyama*

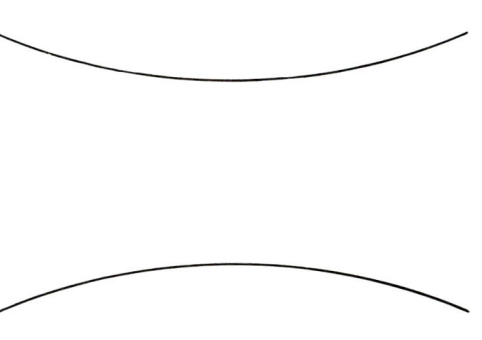

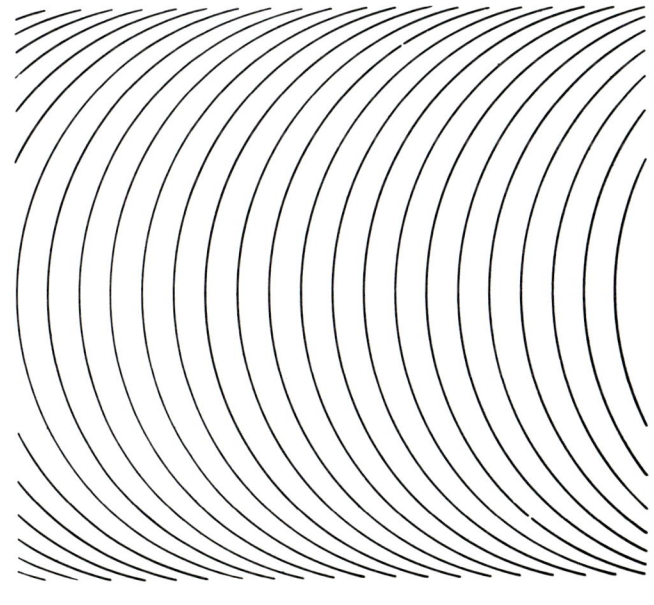

(b) *Orbison Variant*

2.2.9 (a) *Orbison Variant*

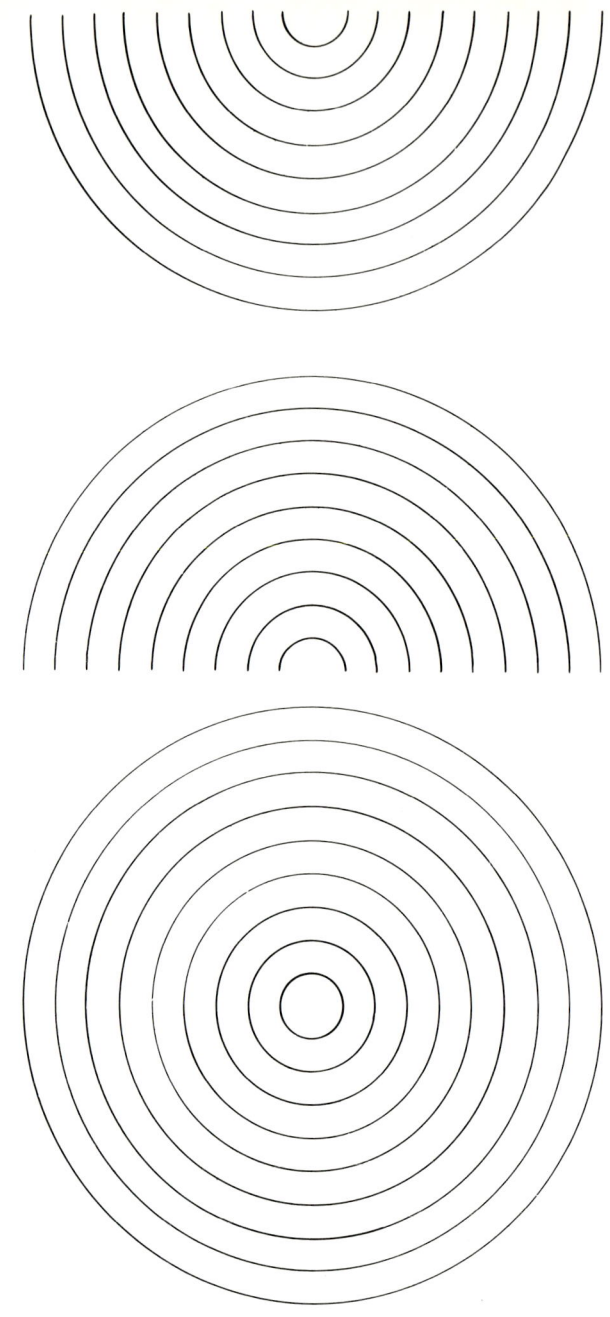

(b) *Orbison*

2.2.10 (a) *Hering*

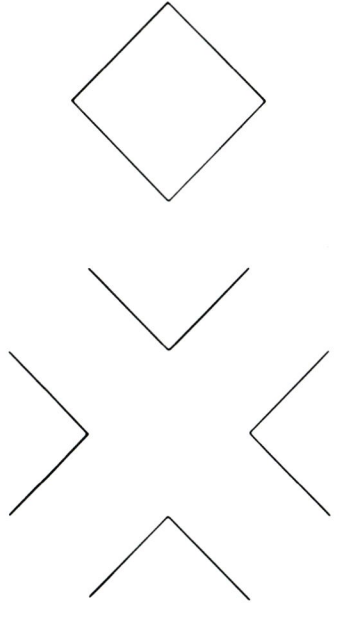

(b) *Lipps*

2.2.11 (a) *Münsterberg*

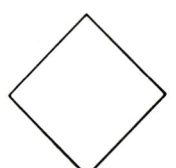

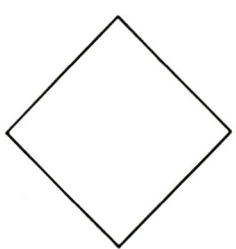

(b) *Wundt*

2.2.12

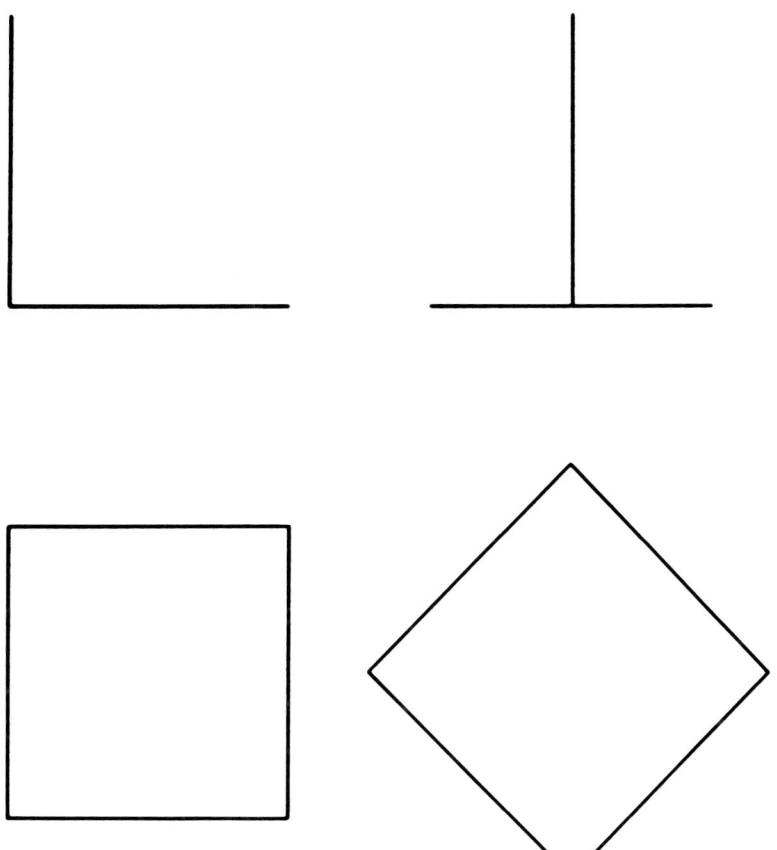

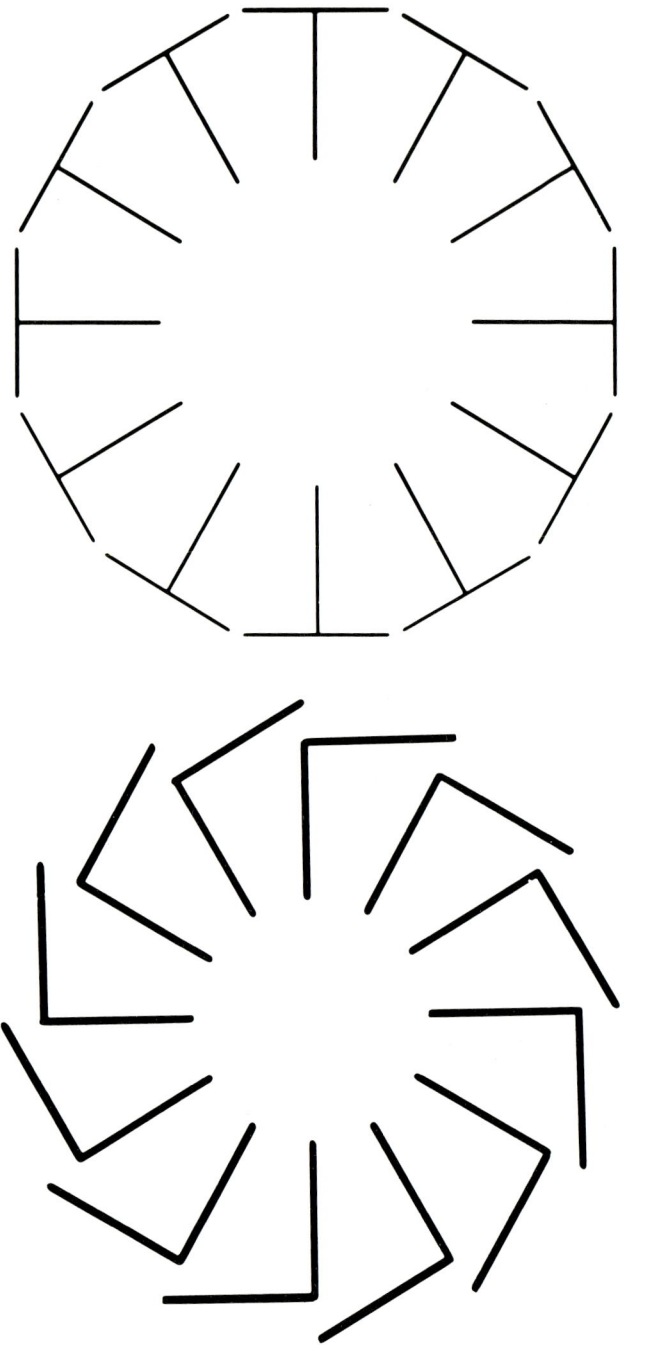

2.2.15

2.2.16

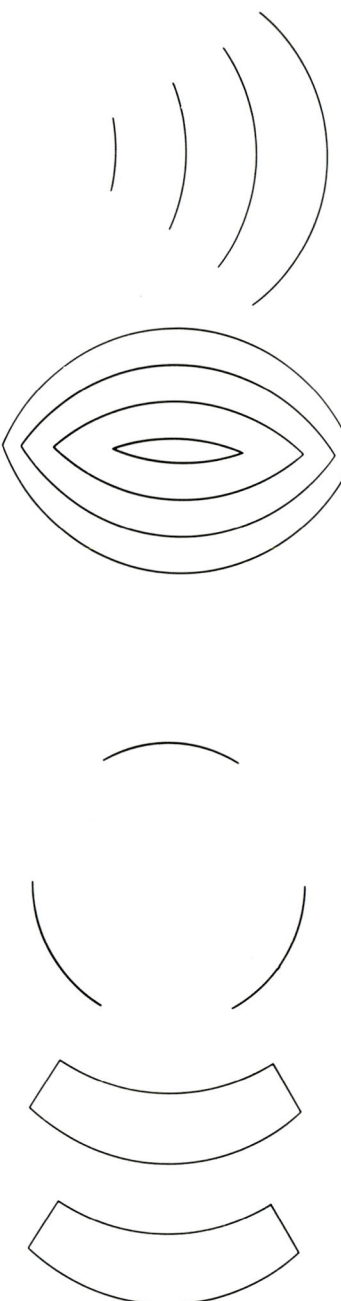

2.2.17

2.2.18

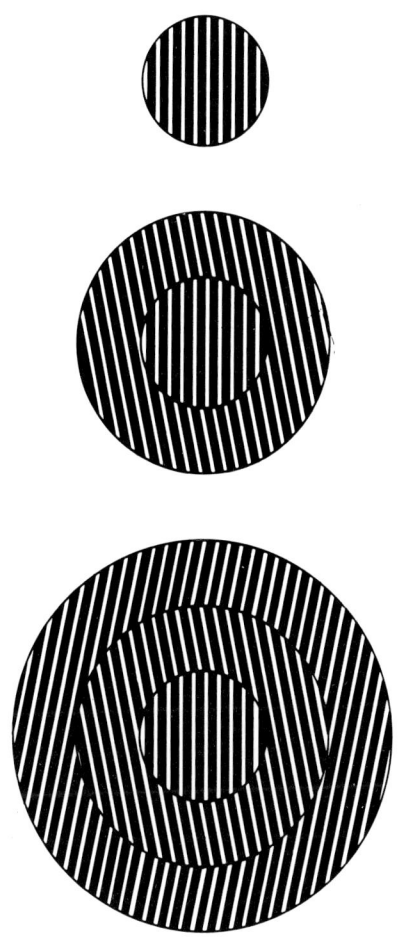

2.2.19

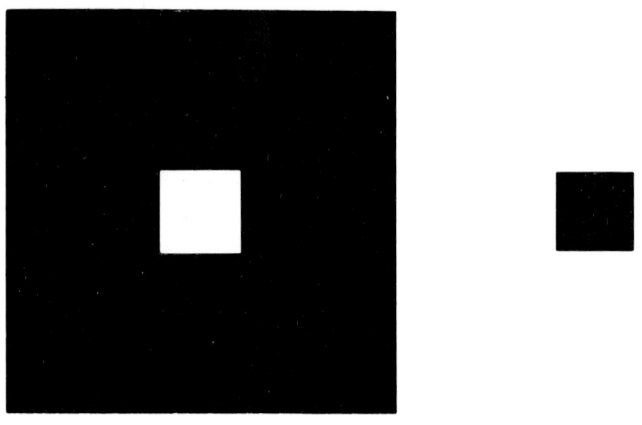

2.2.20

2.2.21

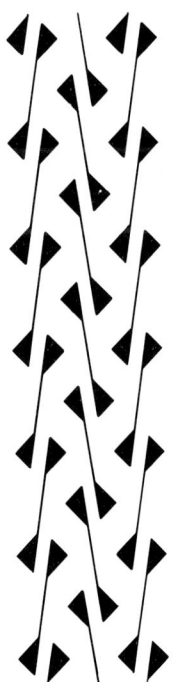

2.2.22

2.3 Theories of illusions

The absence of any clear way of classifying illusion figures does not auger well for theories of illusions. Classification is usually a precursor of interpretation. The scheme that is often implicitly assumed is that illusions involving distortion of a single dimension, like the length or orientation of lines, will prove more amenable to study than those involving more complex distortions, like shape. Indeed, it is in the context of these one-dimensional distortions that most theories have been framed. That is, the grouping of illusions into those of extent and orientation has influenced the theories advanced.

One approach has sought to find processes that vary in a manner equivalent to the perceptual distortions. For example, if the perception of line length or orientation can be associated with the length or direction of eye movements then the illusions could be interpreted in terms of eye movements.[13] Note that this is essentially a redescription of the illusions. In order for it to be an adequate explanation of illusions some statement regarding the manner in which the extent and direction of eye movements are coded into perceived length and direction would be required. At present we have no clear idea of how such coding might be achieved. In fact, theorists supporting eye-movement interpretations have not been consistent in the aspect of eye movements considered relevant to perceptual judgments even of line length. For instance, in the Müller-Lyer illusion it is argued that the arrowheads influence the *extent* of eye movements, so that they actually move further in the upper than in the lower versions of *2.2.1*. However, in another illusion of length, the vertical-horizontal illusion (*2.2.12*), there is little to influence the extent of eye movements and so it is argued that the *effort* to move the eye vertically is greater than that for horizontal movements. Is it the extent or the exertion of eye movements that could mediate perceived length?

The virtue of eye-movement theories is that they are testable; their sorrow is that they usually fail the tests. Illusions can be presented for very short durations, less than one-tenth of a second, so that the eyes cannot move during their presentation. Under these conditions the illusions still occur. The illusion figures can also be stabilized on the retina, by some appropriate optical device or as an after-image, so that the pattern moves with the eye.[14] The illusions still occur, although it is difficult to measure their magnitude under such conditions.

It may well be that eye-movement theories have been proposed precisely because they are measurable. The other processes discussed below have a greater tenacity for the opposite reason — they are not directly measurable. However, before treating them a little more should be said about eye movements. Recent technological advances have increased the precision of their measurement and have greatly increased our knowledge of their complexity.[15] In one sense, this technical sophistication has been matched by the theoretical ingenuity applied to making eye-movement interpretations also essentially untestable. It has been argued that it is not the eye movements themselves, but the *tendency* to make them (or the neural tendency signals called efferent readiness) that determine the illusions.[16] While it is possible to measure eye movements, finding an index of eye-movement tendencies seems more problematical!

Quite a different approach has been taken with a subclass of one-dimensional illusions — those involving distortions of orientation. Here a physiological interpretation is given, for which a little background is necessary. Recent years have witnessed an explosion in our knowledge of visual neurophysiology, due in large measure to the work of Hubel and Wiesel.[17] Starting with cats and then progressing to monkeys they have been able to record the electrical activity of single cells in the visual cortex, and to find the types of patterns that most excite these cells. The 'trigger features' for the cortical cells are edges or lines in specific orientations. Other features of the stimulus are extracted like direction of motion, colour and whether the edges are present in both eyes. It is not known what functions these orientation detectors serve in cat or monkey vision, although speculation abounds. That is, it is not clear whether they are involved in the perception of orientation. Moreover, it is not known whether similar feature detectors are present in the human visual cortex, but it is generally assumed so because the neuroanatomy of our visual system is similar to that of the monkeys examined. The lack of knowledge concerning the functions served by these cortical nerve cells has not inhibited the development of theories of orientation illusions incorporating them.[18] Neural inhibition has, however, been a central feature of the theorizing: the orientation illusions could be due to inhibitory interactions between the orientation detectors stimulated by the distorting and distorted contours. The common descriptive component of orientation illusions is that acute angles (particularly those less than 45°) appear to be larger than they are, i.e., they are apparently expanded, as is evident in the illusions shown in *2.2.5* to *2.2.10*. The suggestion is that the apparent angle expansion is a consequence of inhibition between orientation detectors stimulated by the lines in the configuration.

This theory seems at first sight to be founded on much firmer ground than the eye-movement theories but such is not the case since both suffer from the same deficiency, namely the absence of any explicit evidence regarding the manner in which perception is coded in terms of the mechanisms proposed. The term 'orientation detector' is potentially confusing, as orientation can be taken to refer at one and the same time to an aspect of the stimulus and also an aspect of its perception. It is known that visual cortical cells are excited most strongly by stimulus orientation, but it is an inference that they are involved in the perception of orientation. On this point there is no direct evidence. What is generally assumed is that the peak of some distribution of activity in a population of cortical orientation detectors defines perceived orientation. It is further assumed that the peak is shifted by inhibitory neural interactions to yield the orientation illusions. At present, the evidence supporting this theory is correlational. That is, the tuning characteristics of the orientation detectors (the range of orientations over which they can be excited) are not dissimilar to those for the illusions.[19] However, the occurrence of orientation illusions in figures lacking any intersecting contours is an embarrassment for detector theories: the gap between the lines in *2.2.5a* appears to be expanded to the left. Many other examples of angular distortions of subjective contours have been given by Gregory.[20] Aspects like these render any simple relationship between neural interaction and orientation illusions difficult to sustain even at the correlational level.

A third major theory of illusions stresses the perspective cues that could be present in many of the figures.[21] It is argued that the pictures are initially converted from two-dimensional drawings to represent three-dimensional scenes, and then the judgments of apparent size are determined by apparent distance. For example, the converging lines in the Ponzo illusion (*2.2.2a*) could be a roadway or rail track receding into the distance. If they are so judged then the upper line would be apparently more distant than the lower one. However, they both project equally long images onto the retina. The only way that equal retinal projections could be produced by two lines at different distances is if the apparently more distant one was apparently larger — which is the direction in which the illusion occurs. Similar reasoning can be applied to the Müller-Lyer illusion; the fins can be interpreted as the corners of a room viewed from the inside or the outside. Another perspective cue, that of foreshortening, can be applied to the vertical-horizontal illusion (*2.2.12*). The vertical line can be interpreted as a foreshortened horizontal line receding into the distance, whereas the horizontal line will be judged as at a constant distance; once more, the apparently more distant part is perceived as longer.

The perspective theory is at a different level of explanation to the others mentioned so far. It does not propose any mechanism for the perception of, say, length but relates the illusions to conditions under which length is usually judged accurately — that is, in size constancy. Size constancy refers to the fact that the size of objects is normally perceived in terms of their physical size rather than the size they project on to the retina. If judgments were dependent upon retinal size then an object would appear to reduce its size by half when doubling its distance away. Thus, objects are judged with relative constancy although we do not understand precisely how such judgments are mediated.[22] According to one view cues for the distance an object is away are used to compensate for the varying retinal size. The illusions then become instances of applying the compensatory processes inappropriately.

Because the perspective theory is founded on such a well-established principle as perceptual constancy it has attracted a great deal of experimental interest. This has consisted mainly of devising instances of illusions in which no obvious perspective features are present, but in which the illusions still occur. For example, the Müller-Lyer illusion still occurs with concave and convex semicircles added to the lines, but the semicircles do not provide an impression of perspective depth. Many other instances have been demonstrated.[23]

These critical examples are directed at the perspective features of the illusion configurations. More broadly based constancy interpretations are not so reliant on perspective, but on all the distance cues enlisted in making size judgments.[24] For instance, the relative size of elements, their separation, density or clarity could all be used to provide information for relative distance. In the case of the Müller-Lyer illusion the common feature distinguishing the two parts is that the separation of the extremities (fins, arrow-heads, semicircles or whatever) is greater in the overestimated than in the underestimated component. Indeed, the illusion is comprised of two parts, one with outgoing fins and the other with inward-directed fins, and they are not symmetrical. The figure with the outward-directed fins (with the ends in close proximity) produces a larger illusion than that with inward-directed fins, when they are both judged against a line in isolation. According to the broader-based constancy theory, any cue that can be shown to influence judgments in size constancy would also produce size illusions in two-dimensional drawings. The attraction is not only that the theory addresses more complex cues to size than perspective but also that it potentially encompasses a far wider range of illusions. Shape and orientation illusions could derive from the inappropriate use of cues normally involved in shape and orientation constancy. This profusion of potential cues can prove an embarrassment when attempting to test the theory. In the absence of independent evidence concerning the cues to constancy present in the illusions the danger of circularity is great: the illusions occur because of inappropriate use of constancy cues in the configurations and the features are cues for constancy because they induce illusions. Constancy-scaling interpretations do not say how illusions occur but relate them to familiar perceptual conditions in which judgments are made with precision.

There are many features about illusions that pose general problems for all the theories presented. First, some illusions are reduced in magnitude with repeated testing. This aspect has been used by some theorists to provide an index of the 'cognitive' component in illusions.[25] That is, they suggest that the reduction in illusion magnitude with practice reflects the strategy applied by the observer when inspecting the figure: with repeated observation the eye movements are said to scan the patterns more accurately so that the inducing lines exert less influence. If the strategy of observation is so changed it is strange that the decrement tends to be restricted to the specific configuration used in practice.[26] Second, various illusions change in magnitude with the age of the observer. The developmental trend is not consistent, showing increases with some illusions and decreases with others.[27] Third, certain cultural differences in illusions have been found, though these seem to be relatively independent of the visual environment in which the cultural groups live.[28] It has been suggested that the differences are related to the extent of retinal pigmentation in the eyes of the different groups. Dense retinal pigmentation would reduce the effective contrast of the illusion figures with a consequent decline in the magnitude of illusions consisting of intersecting lines.[29] A similar interpretation has been advanced for the age trends in illusions. Fourth, spatial illusions occur in other sensory modalities. The Müller-Lyer illusion can be induced by pressing an outline of the configuration onto the skin or by tracing over a relief model with the finger tips. All the theories proposed so far have been addressed to visual spatial illusions alone, and could not account for such tactile illusions. Fifth, illusions have been found to occur within many other species like fishes, birds and monkeys, when appropriate testing procedures are employed.

These facts, together with others of greater detail, have led many researchers to abandon the quest for a general theory of illusions.[30] Rather they try to determine the factors involved generally in illusions and to resolve their relative weightings in specific illusions. Thus it is less frequently argued that a particular illusion has a single basis, but that several interacting factors may be involved. In so far as this is the state common to practically all aspects of perception the geometrical illusions join the large band of phenomena awaiting adequate explanation. Accordingly this visual truth has required much study before it has revealed itself to visual illusions!

2.4 Reversing and impossible figures

Certain two-dimensional outline drawings are interpreted as three-dimensional according to the perspective cues contained within them. However, the perspective can be ambiguous so that more than one depth interpretation is possible, and the figures seem to reverse and oscillate between the alternatives. For example, 2.4.1a can be seen as a single cube or as two different cubes, one with the front face directed upwards and to the right and the other with the front face directed downward and to the left. This figure is generally referred to as the Necker cube,[31] after the Swiss crystallographer who described the reversal phenomenon in 1832 (although he represented it in the form of a rhomboid rather than a cube). The remaining three figures in this series — the Mach book (2.4.1b), the Schröder staircase (2.4.2a) and the Beaunis cubes (2.4.2b) — all show similar reversibility of perspective. All are dependent upon the ambiguity associated with the junction of three lines — two obtuse angles and one right angle in the first three and three obtuse angles in the Beaunis cubes.

It should be noted that none of these figures is an accurate perspective drawing. To make them such would reduce or remove the ambiguity. For instance, a cube would project a larger front than rear face and the sides would converge onto the rear face. It is precisely the absence of correct perspective that leads to the oscillations in the figures. None the less, there often are reports of more appropriate perspective features when the cube oscillates — observers often see the more distant face of the cube as larger. This is equivalent to the constancy mechanism that was proposed for illusions; both faces project the same size onto the retina but one is perceived as more distant and is, accordingly, perceptually enlarged. The processes underlying the reversals remain a puzzle. They are not linked in any simple manner to eye movements. Reversals occur with after-images of Necker cubes or when they are viewed as stabilized retinal images.[32] It has been suggested that the eye movements are necessary initially in setting up some schematic representation of the figure in the brain; thereafter, tendencies to make the eye movements are sufficient to induce reversals.[33] This theory is faced with precisely the same problems as those for geometrical illusions invoking eye-movement tendencies, namely, the empirical difficulty of isolating a process for which there is no known dimension of measurement.

A mode of 'explanation' frequently applied to figure reversals, as well as to geometrical illusions, is that of redescribing the phenomenon in seemingly more precise terms. Thus, some sort of switching process between the two alternatives is often proposed, with neural fatigue or satiation reducing the strength of the perceptually dominant one.[34] These inferential processes can only be measured indirectly, and then only when further assumptions regarding their expression have been made. The notion of satiation is inherently plausible, but only because it matches reasonably well with our experience of the phenomenon — it adds very little else.

Reversals in depth also occur with a series of intersecting circles (*2.4.3a*), which can be seen as a cylinder open to the left or to the right. With the crosses in *2.4.3b* the alternation is between a black one on a white ground or the reverse. In this context it is closely related to the figure-ground reversals discussed in section 1.2.

The final group of figures are generally referred to as 'impossible' because the two-dimensional representation could not be realized in three dimensions.[35] That is, the drawings contain accurate perspective features at local junctions, but the various local features do not match globally. For instance, the 'devil's pitchfork' (*2.4.4*) has three prongs at the left but only two rectangular bars at the right! This is possible in a drawing because a cylinder can be represented by two parallel lines and an ellipse whereas a rectangular bar requires three lines. It is impossible only if attempts are made to construct it in three dimensions, although this has not deterred some from trying.[36]

A similar principle applies to the impossible triangle (*2.4.5*). The local features — all the joints — are correctly portrayed, but they could not be connected in three dimensions. Once more, the determined have demonstrated how they can be 'made', although the viewing position is critical for aligning all the parts.[37]

The eternal staircase (2.4.6) was also drawn initially by Penrose and Penrose, but it has had its finest expression in the graphic art of Maurits Escher.[38] He has used these cues to impossibility in a most ingenious manner, and he even animated some of his designs on film.

The fascinating feature about all these figures, both the reversible and the impossible, is the difficulty in seeing them as they are, that is, as flat outline drawings. Their interpretation into three dimensions is primary and immediate, and all the perceptual inconsistencies arise therefrom.

The final three illustrations in this chapter provide a bridge to the next one. Figures 2.4.7 to 2.4.9 complicate the impossibilities by adding curvature, embedding impossible triangles, or by combining two impossibilities within one figure.

2.4.1

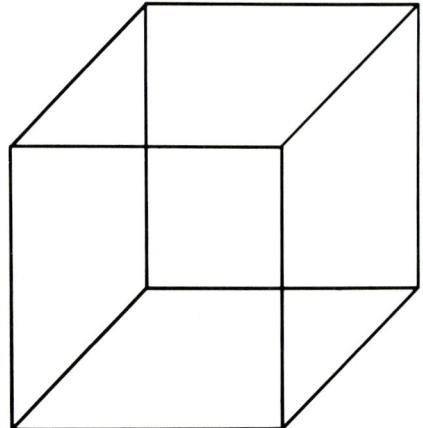

a

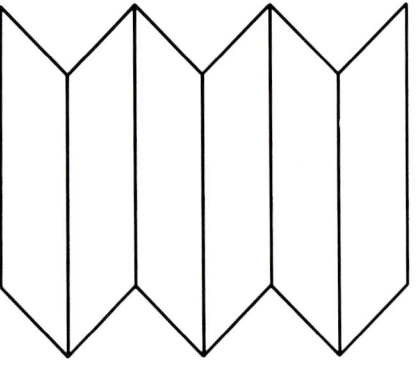

b

192

2.4.2

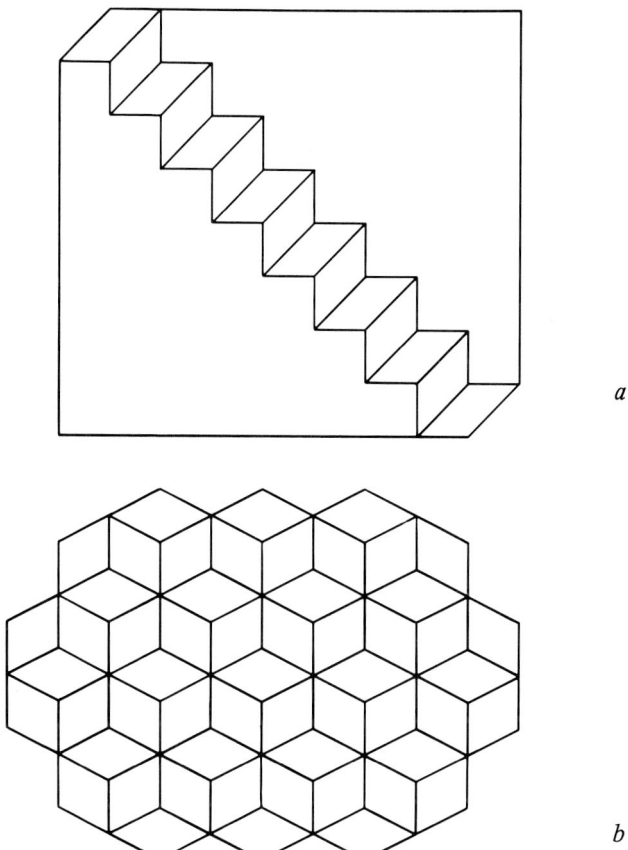

a

b

2.4.3

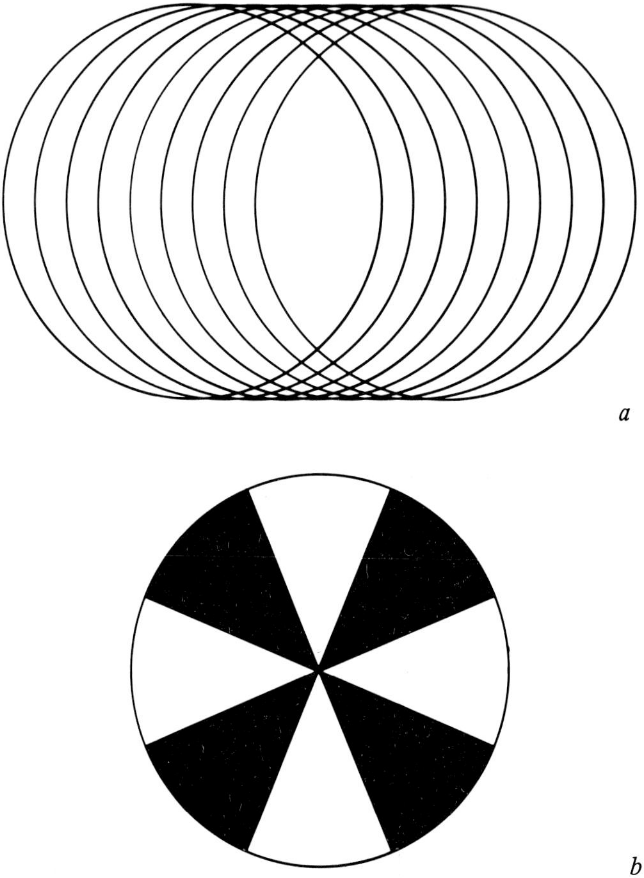

a

b

2.4.4

2.4.5

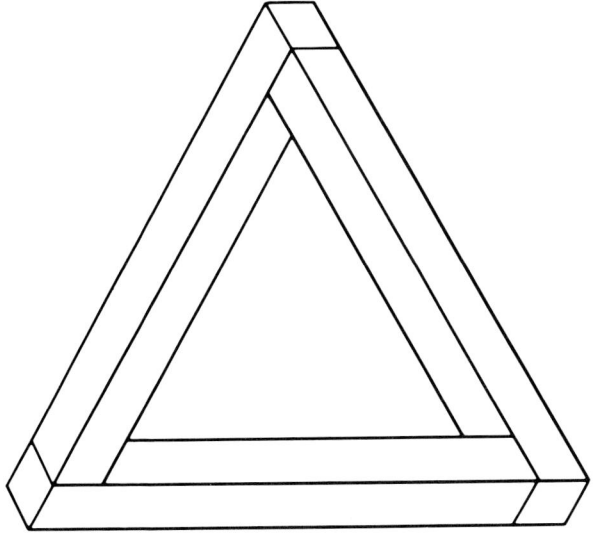

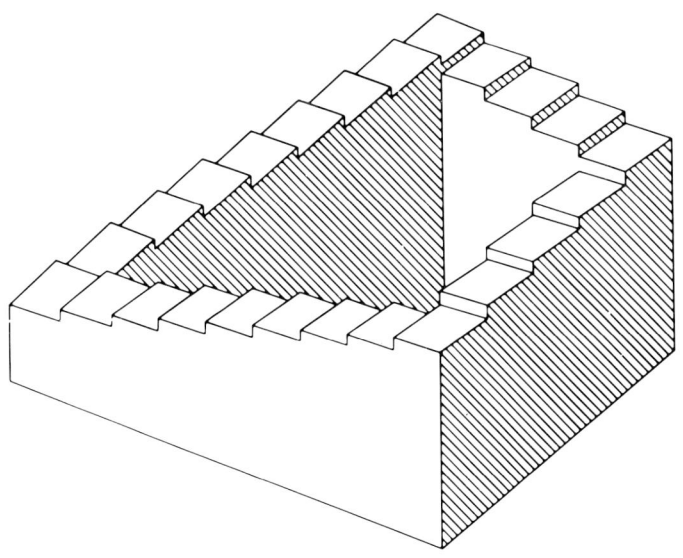

2.4.6

2.4.7

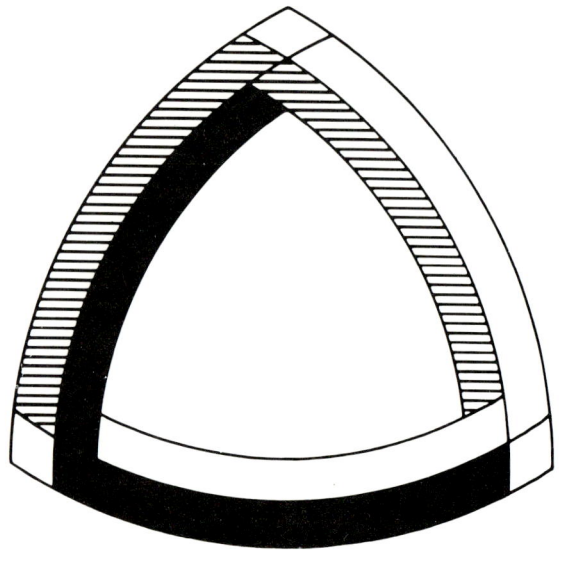

2.4.8

2.4.9

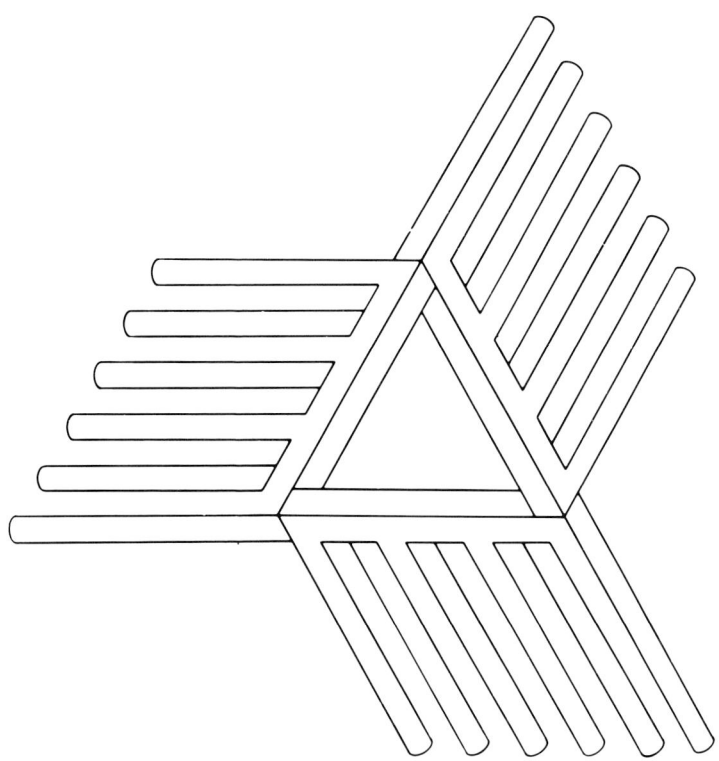

3 Op-tical illusions

3.1 Introduction

The illustrations in this chapter attempt to combine aspects of op designs and of geometrical illusions — hence the title op-tical illusions. The distortions studied under the rubric of geometrical illusions are embedded in backgrounds that can either influence them or generate the variety of op effects discussed in the first chapter. This chapter also contains sections on figure-ground segregation and reversing figures together with a final brief discussion of stereokinetic illusions. The illustrations should speak for themselves with little need for commentary — though some will, inevitably, intrude.

3.2 Op-tical illusions

The dominant strategy employed by psychologists for unravelling the knot of visual illusions has been systematic simplification. Figures are bared to their inductive essentials and beyond. The aim seems to be to destroy the illusions — to find a figure that would still be considered an instance of Xs illusion but without its occurrence. Needless to say, this has proved exceedingly difficult. The illusions can easily be manipulated but not so readily obliterated. Here no attempt is made to follow the course of illusory destruction, rather they are nurtured in figures that are active in the op sense. That is, they are designed to be op-tical illusions — to show a variety of op aberrations as well as geometrical distortions. There is, of course, no guarantee that this approach towards complexity will succeed where simplicity has failed. It does, however, provide an alternative avenue that offers

Op-tical illusions

hope for solutions and from which useful insights might arise. The first examples will be of illusions of extent followed by orientation illusions and then other miscellaneous ones.

The starting-point is the Ponzo illusion. Two horizontal lines of equal length do not appear so because of the converging lines flanking them. Even fragments of the converging lines suffice to induce the illusion (*3.2.1*). It could be due to the closer proximity of the converging lines to one line, but this seems unlikely because the illusion is still present in *3.2.2*. Alternatively, it could be the perspective cues provided by the converging lines, in which case it is puzzling why it survives the radiations of *3.2.3*, where there would seem to be much more perspective information from the many lines converging towards the base of the figure than from the two fragmentary lines converging upwards. Clearly, there is a problem regarding the specification of perspective cues in drawings which will need to be resolved if the perspective or constancy theories of illusions are to survive. The two converging lines appear to be of vital importance, although they do not have to be actual lines (*3.2.4*). Ponzo also demonstrated how the sizes of circles could be modified perceptually by converging lines.[1] If the circles are defined in terms of perspective surfaces alone (*3.2.5*), then the 'nearer' one appears larger, rather than the reverse as predicted by perspective theory. The converging and perspective cues can be set in opposition as in *3.2.6*: the gradient of perspective provided by the horizontal lines indicates that the base is more distant than the top, which contradicts the converging lines. In a similar manner to *3.2.3* the converging lines would seem to be predominant as the upper circle appears larger. Finally, the four horizontal bars in *3.2.7* not only appear unequal in length but also in alignment.

The Müller-Lyer illusion can similarly be seen in a number of variations (*3.2.8* to *3.2.14*), some of which utilize straight and others curved ends. It is not essential to have a line connecting the ends, as can be noted by comparing *3.2.11* and *3.2.12*. It is possible to determine whether after-images undergo variations in their apparent separation by means of figure *3.2.14*. Fixation upon the black dot on the right for about 30 seconds will generate negative after-images when the gaze is transferred to the small white dot on the left. The black discs are equally distant and appear so during initial fixation. The question is whether they so appear when visible as white discs (negative after-images) during observation of the left side. The after-images may take a few seconds to develop and the eyes should be kept as steady as possible. Viewing the left figure for a similar duration

199

Op-tical illusions

will generate black disc after-images when the dot on the right is fixated. By this means one or other after-image can be maintained by alternating the gaze between the fixation points.

A similar approach can be adopted for the Titchener illusion (*3.2.15*), except here the illusion would operate to vary the apparent sizes of the after-images rather than their separation as in *3.2.14*. Other variations based upon the Titchener illusion are illustrated in *3.2.16* to *3.2.18*. In the last one the circles themselves are illusory in so far as they are produced by subjective contours (see section 1.7). Do they appear to vary in size with the length of the lines that define them?

The orientation illusions provide some of the best opportunities for combining the two areas of distortion. The Poggendorff illusion is taken initially, and it can be seen to be operating when only fragments of lines are visible (*3.2.19*) and when the transversals are themselves distorted by the concentric circles. In the last three examples (*3.2.20* to *3.2.22*) it is of interest to note that the moiré fringes, formed by horizontal and near horizontal lines, are also misaligned. Figures *3.2.23* and *3.2.24* extend Ehrenstein's illusion, so that the curvilinear background distorts the rectangular square or grid patterns superimposed upon them. Variations of the Zöllner illusion are shown in *3.2.25* to *3.2.30*; in the first of these the vertical lines appear to be zig-zag three times on their downward descent, but they remain parallel. This is not the case for *3.2.26* in which the parallel lines appear to converge and diverge. Hering grid dots can be seen at the intersections of the lines in these last two illustrations. Concentric squares are either set out of alignment or bent as a consequence of their intersecting lines in *3.2.27* and *3.2.28*. The transparency* provided for *3.2.29* and *3.2.30* enables a simple demonstration of how parallel lines can be systematically tilted or bent; by moving the transparency over the underlying pattern the lines seem almost elastic – they can tilt one way or another and be bent into concave or convex forms. Figure *3.2.29* when viewed alone creates the impression of waves in three dimensions, and the Zöllner illusion is visible in these alone – that is, the waves seem to be diverging or converging according to the orientation of the lines that define them. When the transparency is moved slowly over the waves the lines appear to follow the surface along the peaks and troughs. Finally, *3.2.31* illustrates the distortions of concentric circles when placed upon more densely spaced concentric squares.

* Transparency *3.2*, in the envelope inside the back cover, can be used with figures *3.2.29* and *3.2.30*.

The next set of op-tical illusions involve variations on the Münsterberg illusion. The first illustration (*3.2.32*) returns to the theme of Rubin's figure — the central black rectangles define the outline of profiles or a vase. The horizontal lines do not appear to be parallel, but converge or diverge according to the manner in which the white areas are enclosed by black ones. That is, when a black rectangle encloses part of a white one the white area seems to expand in the manner of the irradiation illusion described in section 2.2; this results in the apparent convergence of the parallel lines. When the figure consists of asymmetries in the overlap of the black and white rectangles then the parallel lines are rotated clockwise in some regions and counterclockwise in others. By modifying the characteristics of the figure — using squares rather then rectangles — as in *3.2.33*, distortions can be induced in both the vertical and horizontal lines. Viewing this pattern for some time results in a remarkable array of orientation distortions. These distortions have proved of some theoretical importance because all the contours in the patterns are at right angles. Other orientation illusions are produced by lines intersecting at acute angles, and it has been suggested that the Münsterberg figures can be similarly described if the centres of the squares or rectangles are connected perceptually. That is, there would be zig-zag elements in the patterns and so the figures might be variants of the Zöllner illusion.[2] However, a number of characteristics of the Münsterberg figures tend to argue against this. First, the illusion is greatly reduced by thickening the lines between the rectangles (*3.2.34*), but this does not reduce the underlying zig-zag pattern. Second, the angle of the 'zig-zags' that produce the largest Münsterberg distortion is around 60°, for which the Zöllner illusion is virtually zero.[3] The magnitude of the Münsterberg illusion varies with the degree of overlap between adjacent rectangles (*3.2.35* and *3.2.36*) and also with the lateral separation of the rectangles (*3.2.37* and *3.2.38*). The involvement of irradiation in the illusion is supported by manipulation of the ratio of black to white areas in the patterns: *3.2.39* is the negative of *3.2.33*, and produces far less distortion. Thus, increasing the ratio of white to black regions increases the illusion. The critical difference between *3.2.33* and its negative (*3.2.39*) would seem to be that of asymmetrical versus symmetrical surround of the white areas. In *3.2.33* the white squares are flanked by two or three black squares, whereas in *3.2.39* every white square is flanked by four black ones. Irradiation can operate in both instances, but it is its asymmetrical expression that is associated with the orientation changes. The examples shown so far all contain lines

Op-tical illusions

separating the component black and white regions. While thickening these lines can result in the disappearance of the illusion, dispensing with them altogether does not, as seen in *3.2.40* and *3.2.41*. Enlisting irradiation as a basis for the various distortions is, of course, adopting a redescription of the phenomenon in terms of a possible mechanism (irradiation) the basis for which remains unknown.

Fraser's twisted-cord illusions are frequently associated with the Münsterberg illusions, and variants of the former are represented in *3.2.42* to *3.2.49*. The first three illustrations are of linear misalignments whereas the remainder are for spirals. Even fragmenting the spirals, so that the constituent parts are generated by subjective contours (*3.2.47* and *3.2.48*), does not destroy the illusion, and it can even be induced by continuous contours, like the radiating faces in *3.2.49*.

The final examples of geometrical illusions blended with op patterns are those in which all the curves are based on arcs having the same curvature, but which appear otherwise because of the variations in arc length over the figures (*3.2.50* to *3.2.52*).

3.2.1

3.2.2

203

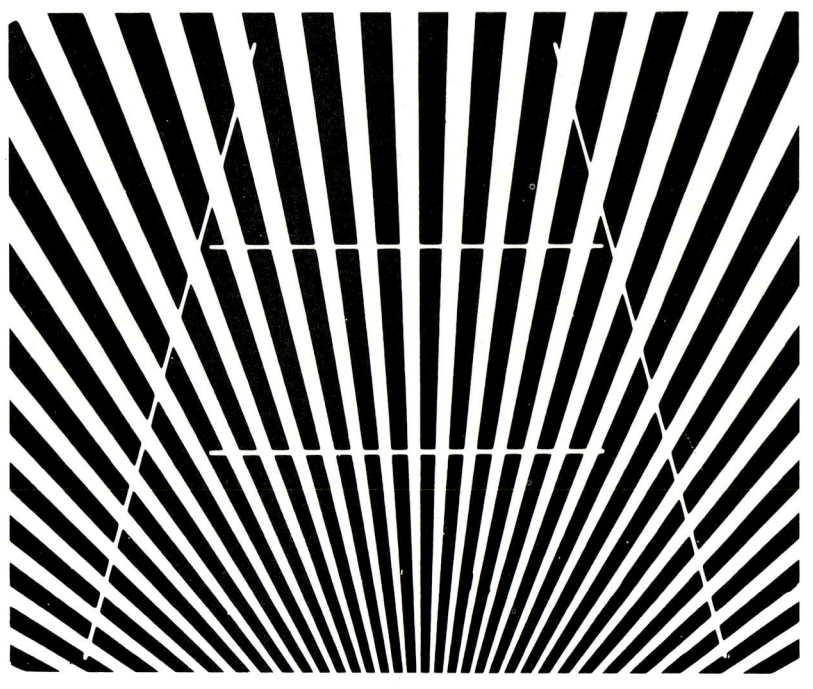

3.2.4

3.2.5

3.2.6

3.2.7

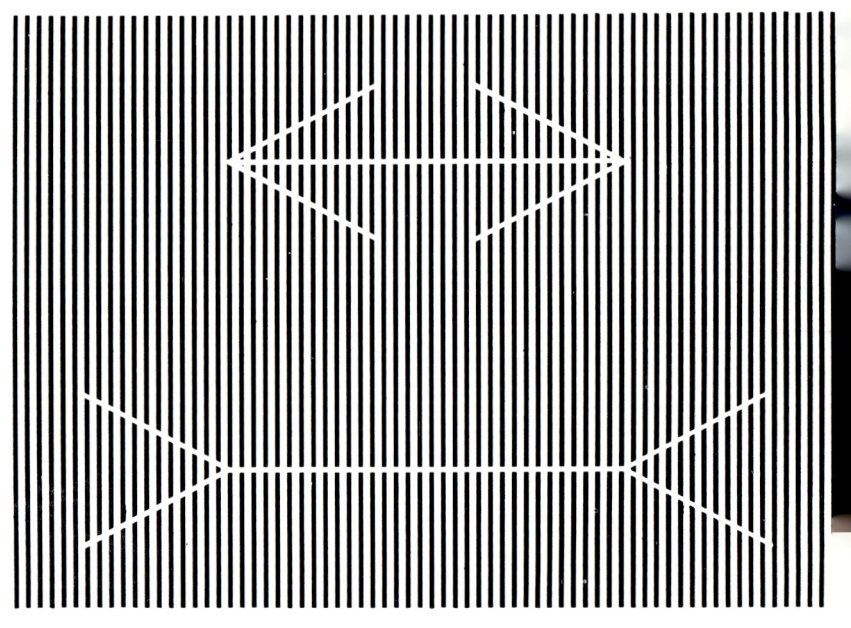

3.2.8

3.2.9

3.2.10

3.2.13

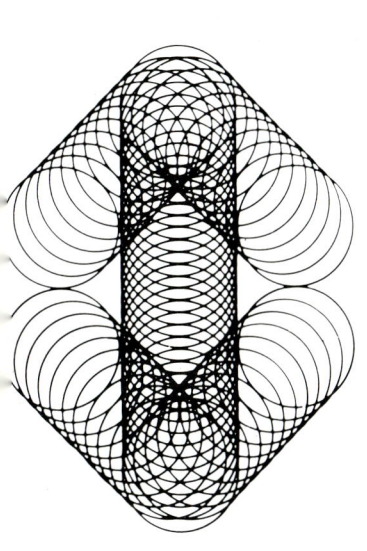
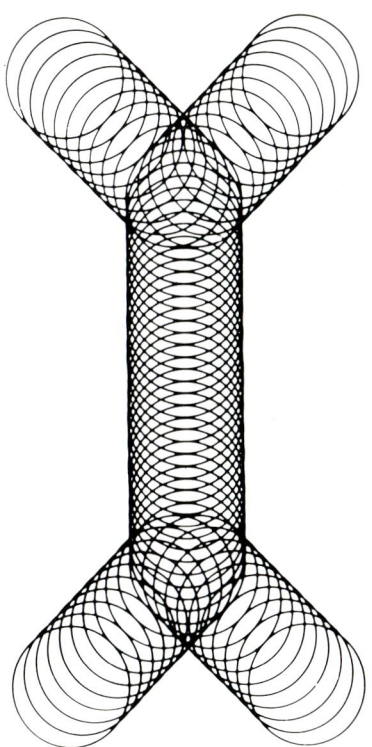

3.2.14

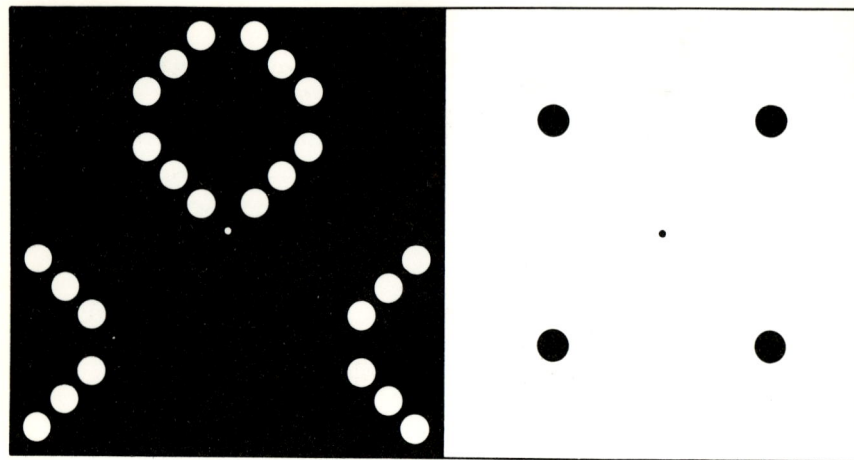

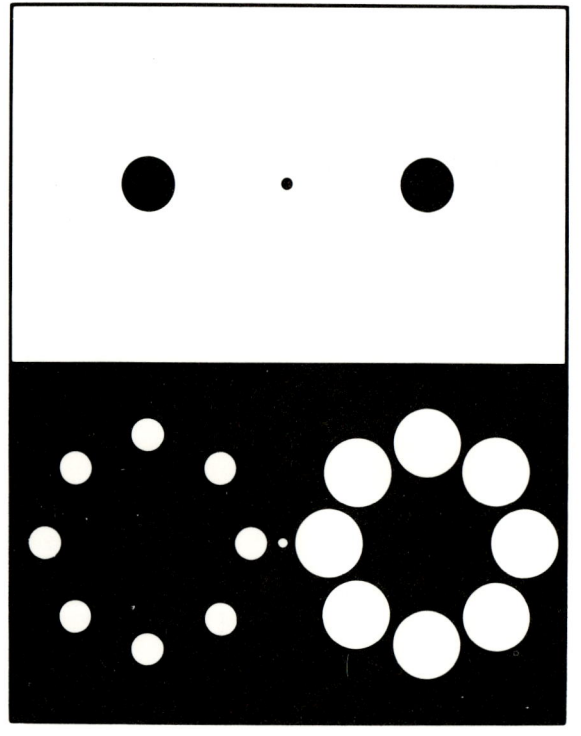

3.2.15

3.2.16

3.2.17

3.2.18

3.2.19

3.2.20

3.2.21

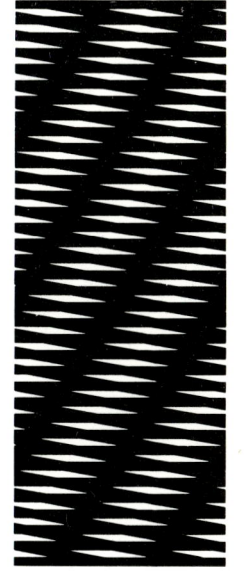

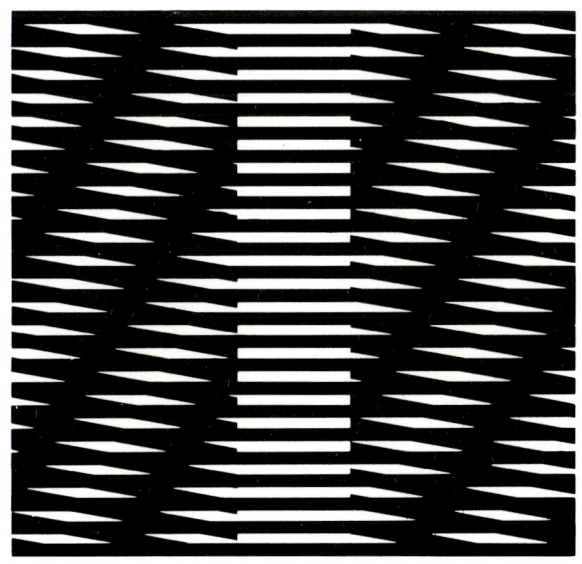

3.2.22

3.2.23

3.2.24

3.2.25

3.2.26

3.2.27

3.2.28

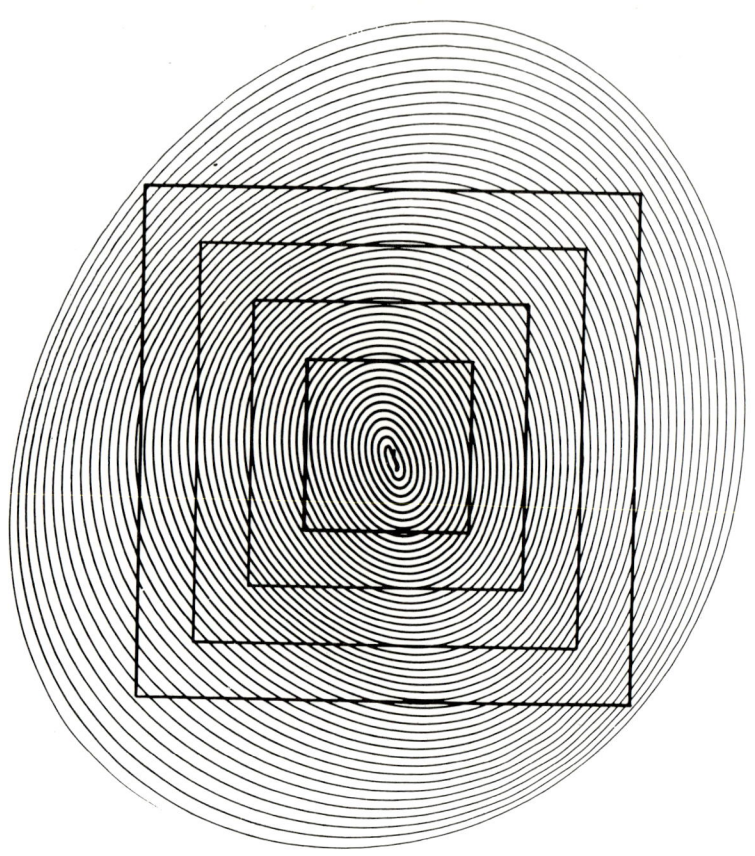

3.2.29

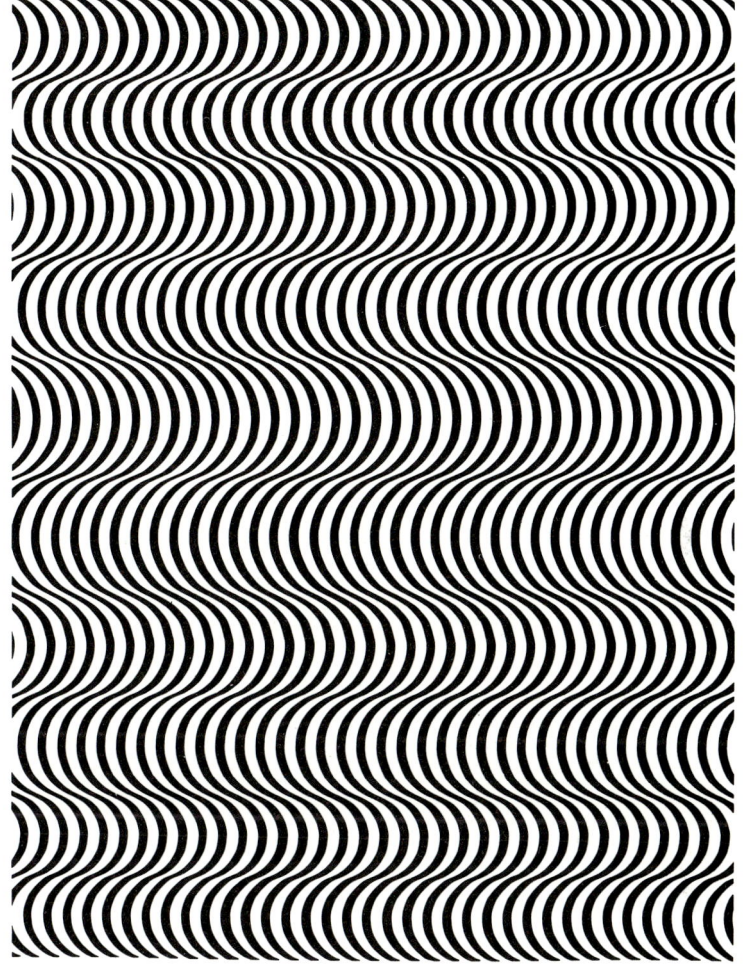

3.2.31

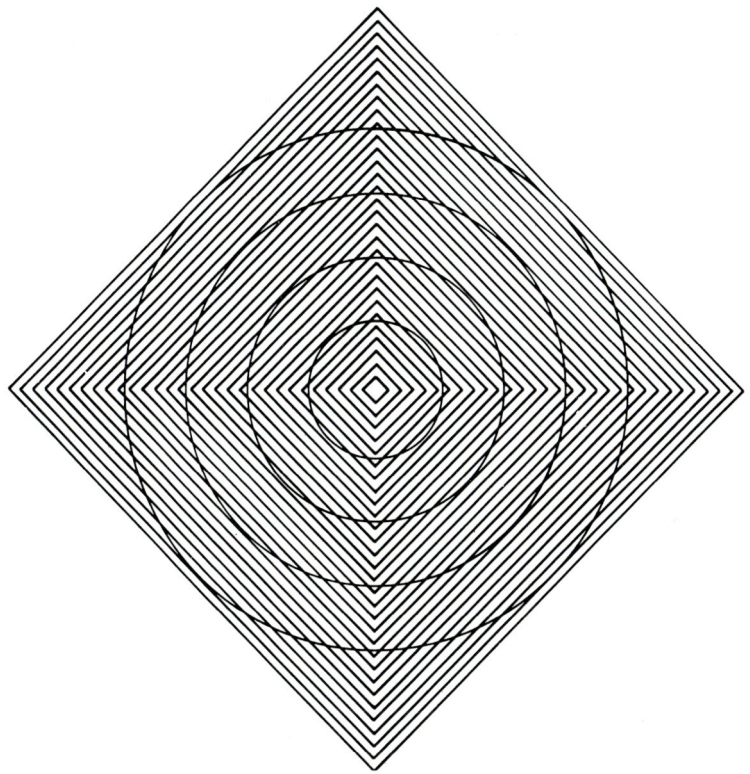

3.2.32

3.2.33

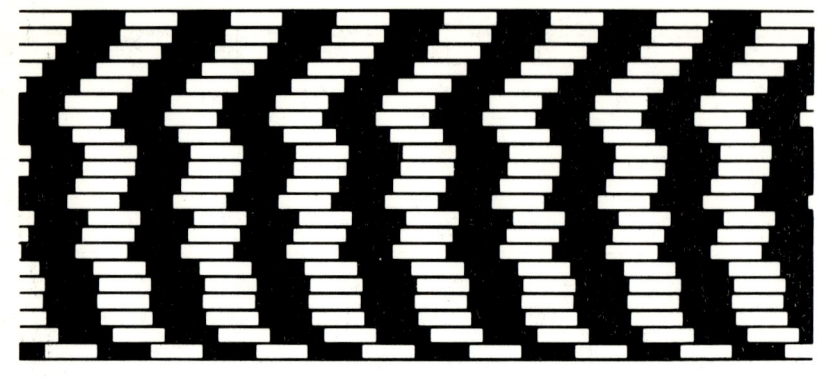

3.2.34

3.2.35

3.2.36

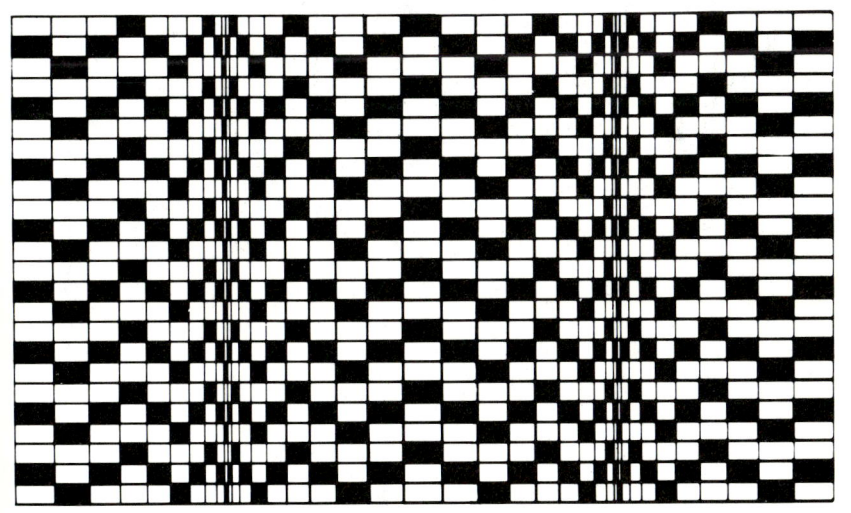

3.2.37

3.2.38

3.2.39

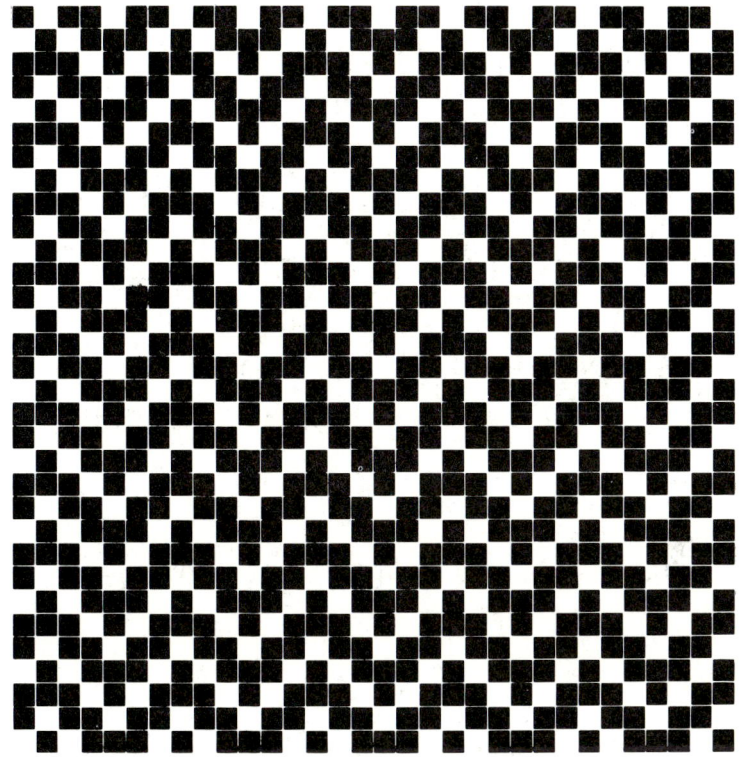

3.2.40

230 3.2.41

3.2.42

3.2.43

3.2.44

3.2.45

3.2.46

3.2.47

3.2.48

3.2.49

3.2.50

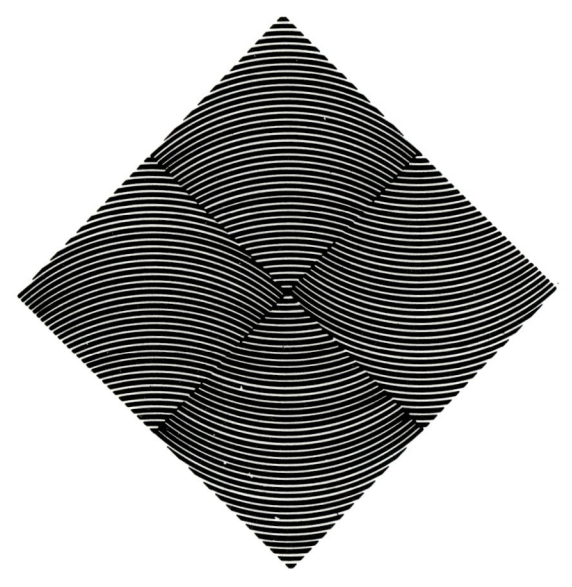

3.2.51

3.2.52

3.3 Reversing figures

This book commenced with illustrations of figure-ground organization and the ambiguities that can be generated in its expression. Particular emphasis was placed on Rubin's demonstration of the reversal in figure-ground perception of the vase/faces design. The first eight illustrations here (*3.3.1* to *3.3.8*) echo those in chapter 1, but the interaction of the figure with the ground is complicated by the introduction of many other contours that are not related to their segregation. Similarly, *3.3.9* to *3.3.11* repeat forms presented earlier in more simplified states (*1.2.25*, *1.2.26* and *1.2.28*, respectively), although their equivalence might not be too easy to trace. In contrast, it is somewhat easier to segregate the Maltese crosses in *3.3.12*.

Perspective reversals can be obtained with the 'block' vase/faces in *3.3.13*. However, since the pattern is not immediately interpretable as a single three-dimensional structure, like the Necker cube, then opposing depth characteristics occasionally emerge for the 'top' and 'bottom' surfaces.[4] This possibility is increased in *3.3.14*, where additional faces are incorporated into the design. The confusion is increased many-fold with *3.3.15*, where it is difficult to segregate the faces prior to combining them in depth, though this latter does remain possible.

The Schröder staircase is shown in *3.3.16* and *3.3.17*. The depth of the stairs can reverse as in the outline version. However, due to the different line orientations in the walls they might appear to differ in clarity because of our slight (regular) astigmatism — in which case the wall with the slightly blurred lines would be interpreted as more distant. Thus, these versions might even be more stable than the outline drawings. Moreover, the walls could have coloured wallpaper because of the subjective colours produced by the gratings!

Reversibilities and impossibilities of depth can be seen in *3.3.18* to *3.3.21*, which are based on the ambiguous cylinder defined by intersecting circles.

3.3.1

3.3.2

3.3.3

3.3.4

3.3.6

3.3.7

246

3.3.8

3.3.9

3.3.10

3.3.11

3.3.13

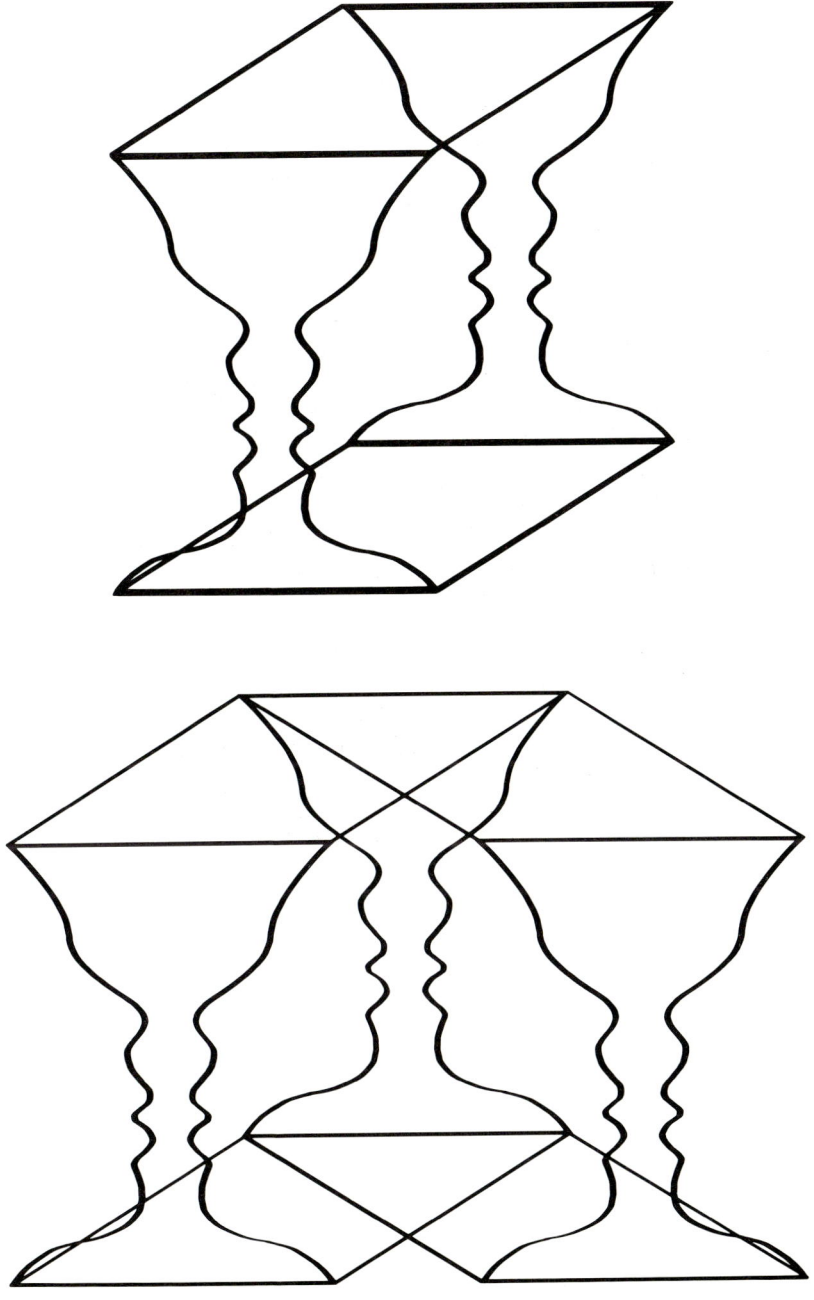

3.3.14

3.3.15

3.3.16

3.3.17

3.3.18

3.3.19

3.3.20

3.3.21

Op-tical illusions

3.4 Stereokinetic effect

Rotating patterns have been employed widely both in visual science and visual art. Marcel Duchamp spanned the two fields with his rotoreliefs, series of slightly eccentric circles which appeared to rotate independently within one another and also looked three dimensional.[5] This appearance of depth with such rotating patterns has been called the stereokinetic effect.[6] The final designs in this section illustrate the stereokinetic effect. They are best observed by placing the centre of the figure over the centre of a record turntable — preferably rotating at 16 or $33\frac{1}{3}$ rpm.

The internal rotation of the circles within one another can best be seen in *3.4.1* to *3.4.3*. The depth characteristics are easier to see when viewing the patterns with one eye. For example, *3.4.4* will appear as two cones attached along one side and rotating around one another. The point of fixation is critical, as is evidenced by *3.4.5*: only the outer white circle that is fixated will take on the independently rotating and depth characteristics.

Finally, rotation of *3.4.6* generates a number of effects: due to the way in which the centres of the circles have been manipulated either narrow spirals contracting towards the centre or broader spirals expanding from the centre can be seen. The narrow spirals correspond to the integration over the fine sections of each 'circle', with the expanding spirals defined by the broader sections of the circles. Record turntables rotate clockwise; if the pattern was rotated counterclockwise then the fine spirals would expand and the broader ones would contract. A strong depth effect is also produced — rather like an unstable vortex boring into or rising up from the plane of the turntable.

3.4.1

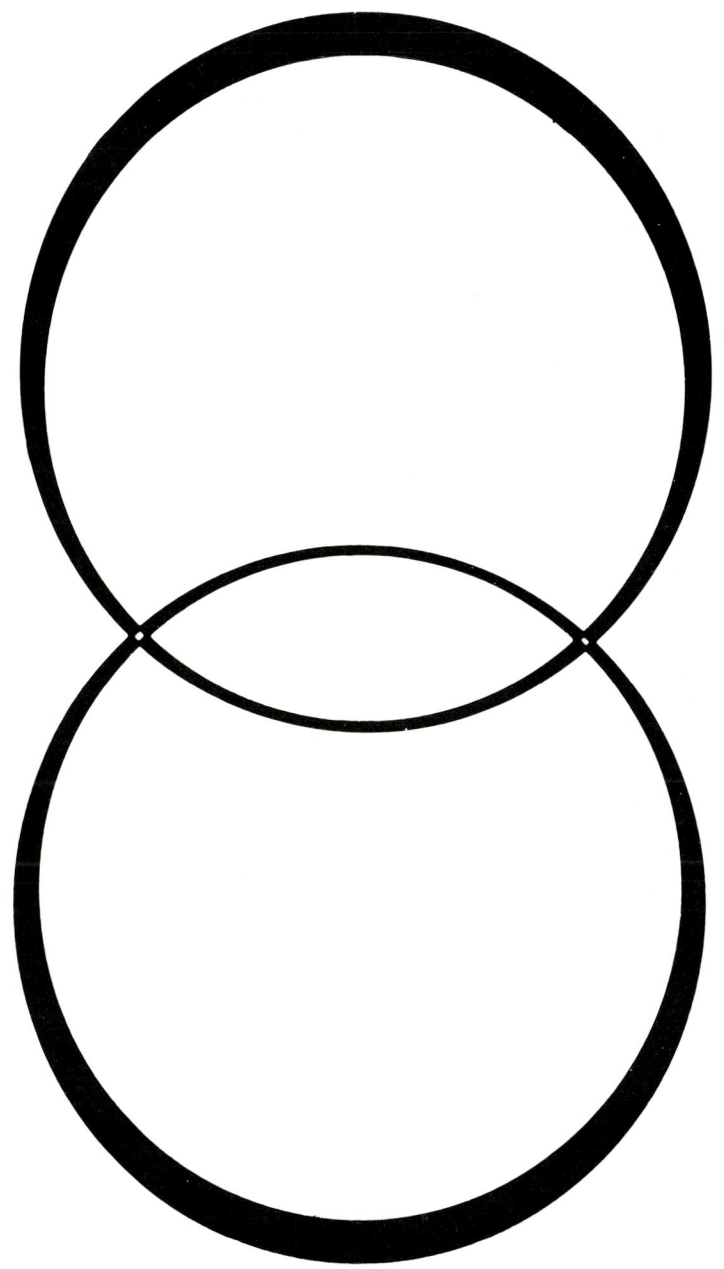

3.4.2

3.4.3

3.4.4

3.4.5

3.4.6

Op-tical illusions

3.5 Conclusions

Artists have frequently adopted the scientists' language, albeit idiosyncratically, to describe aspects of their work. It is less common for scientists to adopt the visual 'language' of the artist to address issues in their own domain. I have tried to follow this second course, that is, to ask questions about the nature of perception graphically. The visual 'language' espoused has been the relatively circumscribed one of Op Art, because within this area there is a close phenomenal commonality between visual science and visual art. Essentially the same phenomena are incorporated into the complex designs of the Op Artists as are analysed in simplified form within the visual laboratory.

The verbal language used to describe Op Art differs radically from that used by the scientist. Indeed, such is the divide that it would often be difficult or impossible to realize that the same phenomena were being discussed. Thus the commonality in phenomena has not been expressed through a common terminology. Throughout this book the verbal language used is more akin to that of science than art, largely because the former is less prone to the ambiguities and intangibilities of the latter. Accordingly, this attempt to span the gulf separating visual art from visual science has adopted the graphic aspects of the former and the language of the latter. To the extent that this endeavour has been in any way successful it will encourage the scientist to consider more complex visual displays and the artist (and, more particularly, the art critic) to develop and use a more circumscribed language – one that assists rather than obscures the bases for their work.

It has been argued above that visual scientists have not adequately represented the subject matter of their own inquiry. The study of perception has been left to artists and the psychologists have become theorists absorbing ideas from related disciplines like neurophysiology and computer science. This flight to other disciplines attests to the difficulty in studying perception scientifically. Thus the visual scientist rarefies phenomena in the controlled conditions of the laboratory; complexity is considered in terms of summing all the isolated effects. On the other hand, the visual artist embraces complexity and, to a large degree, harnesses it. In the context of visual illusions the scientific approach towards simplicity cannot be considered an unmitigated success – rather the reverse. With such a legacy it is not unreasonable to search for insights via pictorial complexity rather than simplicity: the questions addressed can remain simple.

Throughout the book demonstrations have been presented and the

263

readers have been urged to examine their own perceptual experience. No data have been provided to support my descriptions of the illustrations. In this sense the book in general, and the present chapter in particular, can be thought of as old-fashioned. They echo the approach to illusions adopted in the nineteenth century: illusions were not measured but they were demonstrated to occur in this or that configuration. Their detailed measurement is a more recent preoccupation.

It cannot be said that this alternative approach to complicating rather than simplifying illusion configurations has solved the enigma of their occurrence. This remains as elusive as ever. What has been accumulated are more pictorial puzzles that will tax any theory of illusions, but which will be incorporated within any adequate theory. The pictures pose perceptual problems which, hopefully, might spur others to reconsider the nature of illusions and engage in the quantitative approach that I have eschewed. It is also hoped that the pictures might provide some pleasure simply from their perception.

Notes

Chapter 1 Op Art

1 Illustrations of Vasarely's work, particularly those of his formative years, can be found in Vasarely (1965). More recent examples are reproduced in Vasarely (1973).
2 Many books on modern art make passing reference to Op Art, but the two monographs by Cyril Barrett (1970, 1971) provide the most detailed appraisal. The books by the following authors are addressed to the same topic, but vary in the scope of their treatment: Compton (1974), Lancaster (1973), Lucie-Smith (1969), Parola (1969), Popper (1968), Richardson and Stangos (1974), and Seitz (1966).
3 Two of the pioneers of Gestalt psychology, Kurt Koffka (1935) and Wolfgang Köhler (1929, 1940), have written texts describing their approach. Additional source material can be found in Beardslee and Wertheimer (1958), Ellis (1938) and Henle (1961), the first two of which contain many translations into English of original articles written in German. For more recent interpretations of perceptual organization, see Kubovy and Pomerantz (1981) and Kanizsa (1979).
4 See Wade (1978a), where a little history of the phenomena to be discussed is outlined.
5 See Gombrich (1959).
6 These principles were enunciated most precisely by Max Wertheimer (1923), and this classic paper or, more correctly, parts of it have been translated into English (see Beardslee and Wertheimer, 1958, pp. 115-35; Ellis, 1938, pp. 71-88).
7 Rubin's original paper was published in Danish (Rubin, 1915) and would seem to be relatively inaccessible to most students. Fortunately, translations have been published, the most accessible being by Michael Wertheimer (Beardslee and Wertheimer, 1958, pp. 194-203), which is a summary of an earlier German translation.
8 For a preliminary description of stabilized retinal image techniques

265

see Pritchard (1961). A more comprehensive account can be found in Ditchburn (1973).
9 Cognitive approaches of this kind to perception have been proposed by many psychologists, including Gregory (1970) and Oatley (1978).
10 Kandinsky, for instance, makes specific written reference to the importance of line (Kandinsky, 1947), but his pictures are rather easier to comprehend than his text. More general treatments can be found in Arnheim (1954) and Pratt (1979).
11 Victor Vasarely and Bridget Riley have been the most successful exponents of manipulating grouping in abstract designs (see notes 1 and 38).
12 See Ellis (1938) where two articles by Gottschaldt (1926) are translated into English.
13 An excellent introduction to moiré patterns is the booklet by Oster (1964) and his *Scientific American* article (Oster and Nishijima, 1963). Oster is both a scientist and an artist, and his three-dimensional moiré constructions have been widely exhibited and reproduced (see Oster, 1965, 1974). In one of the early critical reviews of Op Art (Lippard, 1967) the supposed sterility of the movement was characterized by the suggestion that the best examples of the genre were produced by a scientist (namely Oster). This uncharitable comment does justice neither to Oster nor to Op Art.
14 The mathematical description of moiré fringes was formulated by Lord Rayleigh (1878). For an alternative view of moirés the reader is strongly recommended to consult the brief biography of one Jean-Baptiste Moiré, in a truly delightful spoof by 'Simplicius' in Weber (1973).
15 The general characteristics of lateral inhibition are depicted in great clarity by Lindsay and Norman (1972). More comprehensive accounts are to be found in Ratliff's (1965) book which contains a translation into English of Mach's classic paper on contrast, and also in von Békésy's monograph in which the process of lateral inhibition is invoked to account for a perplexing variety of phenomena in all sensory modalities.

The eminent neurophysiologist Richard Jung has argued that the neural processes of lateral inhibition are readily expressed by artists' endeavours, particularly in drawing. That is, in commencing with an outline sketch and subsequently adding the subtler shades the artist is reflecting the early processes of contour extraction then their subtle augmentations that occur within the visual system (see Jung, 1971, 1975). My approach to the analysis of art so closely corresponds to that of Professor Jung that I can do no better than quote a passage from his work:

> I am convinced that correlations between natural science and painting may be better understood if one proceeds from visual perception and examines whether or not the artist makes use in

Notes to pages 36-8

his pictures, more or less unconsciously, of abstraction principles similar to those involved in visual processes (Jung, 1975, p. 226).

Where I am somewhat at odds with Professor Jung is that, contrary to his statement, he concentrates on visual physiology rather than visual perception, whereas my concern is with visual perception, rather than neural processes, and art.

16 The curve depicted by the moiré fringes of *1.3.4* corresponds to the lateral inhibitory effects operating within the retina. More specifically, it represents the response characteristics of a retinal ganglion cell to edges placed at different positions with respect to its excitatory centre (see Enroth-Cugell and Robson, 1966).

17 Many contrivances have been designed to depict the path traced by moving bodies; some of the earliest illustrations can be found in papers by Thomas Young (1800) and Charles Wheatstone (1827). The patterns can be produced by combining two simple harmonic motions by means of a universal joint. Reference is made to such a device, with illustrations of its operation, in a text on theosophy by Besant and Leadbeater (1905) — the patterns were considered to represent such thought states as 'An aspiration to enfold all'. The harmonograph consists of a stationary pen that rests on a moving platform, which is supported from above on a universal joint and is counterweighted below. Similar patterns can be generated, at somewhat greater expense, on visual display units under computer control (given suitable human guidance), and some examples can be found in Krantz (1974).

18 See the prints and transparencies enclosed inside the back cover of Vasarely's book (1965).

19 Lord Rayleigh (1878) appreciated the significance of moiré fringes from crossed gratings following the accidental displacement of two transparencies of finely ruled patterns.

20 Detailed treatment of crossed gratings can be found in Guild (1956).

21 Wilding's predominant concern has been with moiré fringes generated by periodic patterns in relief; these are best reproduced in the catalogue to an exhibition in 1973 (Wilding). His subsequent development has been directed to binocular stereoscopic vision, and this is best described in his booklets on vision and perception (Wilding, 1976, 1977). In many respects Wilding's method for generating differential disparities of moiré bands matches the ingenuity of Julesz's random dot stereo pairs (see Julesz, 1971).

22 Photographs of Soto's constructions can be found in Barrett (1970, 1971) and Compton (1974), although the range of his work can best be appreciated from exhibition catalogues (e.g. Soto, 1969; Exhibition Catalogue of Venezuelan Art, 1978). Soto's works do not lend themselves to photographic representation, since they are so intrinsically dynamic. The reader can only be encouraged to see them in their three-dimensional complexity, if the occasion permits.

Notes to pages 73-6

23 If eye movements were the basis for generating the effect then stabilizing the pattern on the eye should obliterate the blurring effect. Such experiments have been conducted, and while the results are not as consistent as might be anticipated, they are most instructive. Using an optically stabilizing device Pritchard (1958) found that the blurring was still visible within a pattern of concentric circles. Using a similar pattern generated as a prolonged after-image, Evans and Marsden (1966) found that the blurring was not reported. Optical stabilization and after-images are generally considered to be equivalent in the perceptual effects they induce (see MacKinnon, Forde and Piggins, 1969), but here the results differ. This outcome is comprehensible when the differences between the two procedures are appreciated: optical stabilization only presents a non-moving image to the eye, not to the retina. Any structure within the eye, like the lens, that can move will vary the characteristics of the retinal image. Such variation due to changes in lens curvature would not influence the after-image, since the image is 'painted on the retina' during the brief discharge of the flash-gun.
24 The developmental changes in the optical characteristics of the eye are described by Duke-Elder (1970), Trevor-Roper (1970) and Weale (1968).
25 Transient variations in accommodation, which are astigmatic, have been measured by Arnulf and Dupuy (1960) and Campbell, Westheimer and Robson (1959); they vary with a frequency of around 2 Hz. The consequences of transient astigmatism for the appearance of regular repetitive patterns have been clearly described by Millodot (1968).
26 This problem was associated with MacKay's (1957) report of distortions in radiating patterns of lines. Campbell and Robson (1958) found that the distortions did not occur when a small (1mm) artificial pupil was used, and this was confirmed by Millodot (1968). Helmholtz (1924) had addressed the same question from a different direction and came to a similar conclusion. Viewing a pattern of concentric circles he observed radiating and rotating 'spokes', but their number and degree of rotation decreased with increased viewing distance (and, thus, decreased accommodation). He attributed this to some 'asymmetry of the eye', namely, astigmatism.
27 Astigmatism was measured originally by Thomas Young (1801) for his own eyes, and its more detailed characteristics have since been elucidated (see Duke-Elder, 1970). The consequences of astigmatism for optical image formation are described in detail by Pirenne (1970).
28 See Duke-Elder (1970, p. 282). In most cases of astigmatism each eye has the same axis of blurring.
29 Stanley and Hoffman (1976) reported this colour phenomenon and suggested that it was related to the colour-contingent after-effects described initially by McCullough (1965). A thorough review of these colour-contingent after-effects can be found in Stromeyer (1978).

Notes to pages 76-7

30 The extent of chromatic aberration in the eye is described in most text books on physiological optics (see Davson, 1972; Duke-Elder, 1970; Helmholtz, 1924). More specific aspects with respect to art are discussed in the article by Ames, Proctor and Ames (1922).
31 See the delightful essay by Helmholtz (1881) on the eye as an optical instrument, which essay is part of a broader lecture on the then contemporary state of research on vision.
32 This interpretation of Stanley and Hoffman's colour-effect has been proposed both by Wade and Day (1978) and by Hohmann and Malsburg (1978). Positing the perceived colour in the optical characteristics of the eye renders other aspects of the effect more readily interpretable. For example, the contours appearing a particular colour are reversed when the head is tilted by $90°$, and the colours are not so readily visible for concentric squares oriented obliquely. Both of these effects would be predicted if the colours were generated by astigmatically determined chromatic aberration, the axis of which is generally vertical or horizontal.

It is also possible that chromatic aberration is implicated in the colour-contingent after-effects mentioned in note 29. The McCullough effect consists of alternately presenting, say, vertical black and orange stripes and horizontal black and blue stripes. After several minutes of such alternation a black and white pattern made up of vertical and horizontal stripes appears delicately coloured so that the white verticals appear blue-green and the horizontals orange. Various interpretations of this after-effect have been proposed (see Stromeyer, 1978). It remains possible that chromatic aberration could be involved in it, too. During the inducing period the orange vertical will require a different state of lens curvature for its focus than that for the blue horizontals. Thus, during the inducing phase pattern-selective states of accommodation are alternating. Suppose that this alternating sequence induces a conditioned relationship between a specific orientation and a specific state of accommodation. When the black and white test pattern is presented one of the orientations, the vertical, say, will invoke the state of lens curvature previously associated with it (orange). Since the pattern is black and white, the white light will be dispersed according to the aberrant properties of the eye: when the eye is accommodated for orange with vertical lines this will enhance the aberration of the shorter wavelengths, and vice versa for the horizontal stripes. Only one such state of accommodation could be achieved at any moment, so the colour induced in one set of contours due to chromatic aberration could in turn induce the complementary colour in the other lines by simultaneous contrast. At the very least, this type of interpretation would require rejection before more complex processes, like colour-coded cortical edge-detectors, are invoked.
33 The accidental observation of pastel colours with black and white patterns has occurred so frequently that no fewer than a dozen

269

'discoveries' of it have been reported in the literature (for their history see Cohen and Gordon, 1949; Erb and Dallenbach, 1939; Wade, 1977a). The most common occurrence has been with rotating black and white patterns. Many different arrangements of the black and white areas have been devised so that different colours can be seen at the same angular velocity (see Robinson, 1972, p. 247 for the different discs that have been used). However, colours can be seen in finely striped stationary patterns, and it was following observation of one such — in fact an engraving of a map in which the sea was represented as fine parallel lines — that Brewster (1825) first reported the phenomenon.

34 The dots often appear in many colours and seem to dart and dance over the inducing pattern (see Wade, 1977b). Similar dancing dots can be generated if a patternless surface is flickered at a frequency below that of critical flicker fusion (see Brown and Gebhard, 1948; Purkinje, 1823).

35 Many independent descriptions of the streaming effects have been given, and these are tabulated, together with other distortions seen in geometrically periodic patterns, in Wade (1977b).

36 As with the allied phenomena described in note 35, this after-effect has frequently been 'discovered'. Perhaps Purkinje (1823) was the first to give it a precise description, but more detailed characteristics have been described by Pierce (1901), MacKay (1957) and Georgeson (1976a, 1976b). A translation of Purkinje's original report can be found in Ripps and Weale (1976).

37 It is not uncommon for art critics to use phrases like 'art that assaults the retina' and 'art that attacks the eyes'. Certain individuals do find it disturbing to look for long at Op Art works, as they can sometimes induce headaches. Indeed, there is some similarity between the visual distortions described above and the 'fortification illusions' reported prior to a migraine attack in some sufferers (see Airy, 1870; Richards, 1971; Wade, 1978a).

38 Bridget Riley's early work has been summarized in the well-illustrated book by de Sausmarez (1970), and in articles by Robertson (1971) and Thompson (1971). Riley's more recent work is best seen in catalogues to her exhibitions, one of which is a major retrospective of works from 1959-78 (Riley, 1978).

39 An introduction to after-images can be found in Brown (1965); Wade (1978b) discusses characteristics of long-lasting patterned after-images, which undergo phases of fragmentation, disappearance and reappearance before they finally fade from view.

40 Surveys of research on human colour vision can be found in Boynton (1979), Hurvich (1981), Kaufman (1974) and Mollon (1979, 1982).

Helmholtz (1924) showed that there are two methods of colour mixing, which are referred to as additive and subtractive. Additive colour mixing applies to the combination of different light sources and the primaries correspond to red, green and blue. This seems to approximate the way colours are combined visually, and the subsequent discussion assumes this. When all three primaries are mixed additively white light is produced. Pigments, when mixed, follow different rules — they combine subtractively. Thus, mixing the three primaries (corresponding to red, yellow and blue) yields black rather than white. Pigments absorb most of the light falling on them and the wavelength reflected defines the colour perceived. When two pigments are mixed the ensuing colour corresponds to the common wavelengths reflected by each of them.

41 *White Discs I* can be seen in reproduction in Riley (1978) and Wade (1978a, p. 26).

42 This method of observing the consequences of our own involuntary eye movements was devised by Verheijen (1961). The negative after-image that is superimposed on the grid will appear to drift slowly for short periods, then flick to another position. In addition to these drifts and flicks there is a very high frequency tremor, but its amplitude is so small that it is unlikely to be noticeable. (See Alpern, 1972, and Carpenter, 1977, for a discussion of involuntary eye movements.)

43 Many books on colour provide very few coloured illustrations, and these rarely reflect the variations and subtleties of our colour perception. This might be occasioned, in part, by the difficulties (and expense) of precise colour specification in printing, although some successful examples do exist. The book by Marx (1973) is particularly good for presenting examples of simultaneous contrast and subtractive colour mixing. In the case of the former, apertures in pages are provided so that the exposed colours can be compared with and without variously coloured surrounds. This is especially useful in teaching as it is not uncommon for students to entertain the notion of chicanery on behalf of the teacher when told that two discriminable colours are physically identical. The distrust is then displaced from the teacher to the senses. Hurvich's (1981) book gives a lucid account of colour phenomena and deficiencies from the standpoint of the opponent-process theory of colour vision. This theory was formulated in the last century by Ewald Hering and it has been elaborated and extended by Hurvich and his colleagues. For a more individual approach to colours and their classification, see Itten (1961).

44 Uttal (1978) addresses the problems posed by relating the perceptual effects of simultaneous contrast to possible underlying neural mechanisms. See Uttal (1981) for a more general critique of attempts to reduce perceptual phenomena to neurophysiological processes.

45 The 'fluttering hearts' phenomenon was reported by both Wheatstone and Brewster at a meeting of the British Association for the Advancement of Science in 1844. Wheatstone gave the initial description, as he had observed it when viewing a red and green carpet in gas light. Brewster then recorded how it was often drawn in red and blue and depicted in the shape of hearts. Marcel Duchamp has developed this theme further with a design, called

Fluttering Hearts, which encloses hearts in alternating red and blue (see Barrett, 1970, p. 24 for an illustration of this).

46 More detailed analyses of the fluttering hearts phenomenon can be found in von Grünau (1975) and Robinson (1972). The colour combinations that yield the fluttering heart phenomenon are typically those involving saturated colours of approximately equivalent luminance. It has been found that such combinations (referred to generally as isoluminant) pose particular problems for accommodation, i.e., the edges cannot be focused (see Wolfe and Owens, 1981). Accordingly, it is possible that the pulsations and apparent movement that occur with such stationary patterns might reflect the marked variations in chromatic aberration that would be consequent upon large and uncontrolled changes in accommodation.

47 The illusory dots were initially described by one Rev. W. Selwyn and communicated to a meeting of the British Association by Sir David Brewster (1844a). Brewster reported that white dots could be seen at the intersections of black lines on white paper. This later became known as the Hering grid, after Hering described it in 1878. Several years earlier Hermann (1870) had observed the converse phenomenon — black dots appearing at the intersections of white lines drawn on a black background.

48 See Baumgartner (1960) and Jung and Spillmann (1970).

49 Excellent introductions to the anatomy and physiology of the visual system can be found in collections of *Scientific American* articles (Held and Richards, 1972, 1976; Hubel and Wiesel, 1979) and in Frisby (1979).

50 This interpretation was proposed initially by Baumgartner (1960) and has been developed by Jung and his colleagues (Jung, 1973; Jung and Spillmann, 1970; Spillmann, 1971).

51 An additional difficulty regards the occurrence of the Hermann dots when the grids are presented dichoptically, albeit with higher thresholds (Lavin and Costall, 1978). That is, if alternate rows of squares are presented to each eye the grid is formed at and beyond the level of binocular combination, which is in the visual cortex. The occurrence of the illusory dots under these conditions would suggest that earlier stages in visual processing, like the retina or lateral geniculate body where receptive fields have concentric configurations, are not the site for their generation. However, Troscianko (1982) has produced evidence from dichoptic experiments which is taken to support a peripheral interpretation of the illusory dots.

52 Jung (1973) and Frisby (1979) have suggested that the receptive field characteristics of the human visual system are tapped directly by this means. These speculations are open to question on several grounds. For example, receptive fields evidence a high degree of overlap throughout the visual system and the extent to which they interact could influence the limiting dimensions of the illusory dots. Furthermore, there is the assumption that the locus of generation of the dots is retinal or lateral geniculate, which assump-

tion has been questioned above (note 51). However, even if the assumption is correct, it is known physiologically that the receptive field information extracted at early levels is radically transformed cortically. How would the discontinuities determining the illusory dots be maintained throughout such transformations?

53 Blakemore (1973) has drawn attention to the operation of Hermann and Hering grid effects in some of Vasarely's paintings.

54 The diagonal components of the checkerboards can also be described in terms of a Fourier analysis of the patterns. Any distribution of luminances can be reduced to a set of components that have sine-wave distributions varying in spatial frequency. That is, a spatial distribution of light can be described mathematically in the same way that Fourier discovered for a temporal distribution of sound waves (see Campbell, 1974; Braddick, Campbell and Atkinson, 1978; Sekuler, 1974; Weisstein, 1980). Thus, patterns can be described in terms of a set of sine-wave spatial frequencies of specific amplitude and phase. In the case of a checkerboard pattern Fourier components lie at $45°$ and $135°$ to the main lines defining the checks, and these approximate the diagonals seen when the pattern is blurred.

55 The implicit emphasis on the analysis of contours can be found in theories of radically different persuasion — e.g. the Gestaltists (see note 3), Hebb (1949), Gibson (1950, 1966, 1979), Attneave (1954) and Marr (1976) Marr and Nishihara, 1978).

56 See Kanizsa (1976) and Schumann (1900).

57 See Coren (1972) and Gregory (1972).

58 See Brigner and Gallagher (1974) and Frisby (1979).

59 This technique has long been used by engravers to provide the suggestion of an overlapping surface. It was described in terms addressed explicitly to perception by Schumann (1900).

60 The stereoscope was initially devised by Sir Charles Wheatstone in the early 1830s, in order to explore certain theoretical problems of binocular vision. Wheatstone's stereoscope consisted of two mirrors, each at $45°$ to the line of sight, so that different patterns could be presented to each eye. The mirror stereoscope was somewhat cumbersome, and it was largely replaced by the lenticular stereoscope of Sir David Brewster, which placed two semi-lenses side by side in order to act both as magnifiers and prisms. Many other contrivances have been developed since, but the majority bear resemblances to Wheatstone's or Brewster's designs. There are, however, other means of separating the images to the two eyes. As early as 1858 a method of projecting two different images through complementary coloured glasses, onto a screen and viewing them with similar glasses, one before each eye, was demonstrated. Later this same idea was expressed on the printed page by using different coloured inks viewed through similarly coloured glasses and it was patented in 1891. The technique was given the name 'anaglyph'.

The fascinating history of stereoscopes, and the controversies

Notes to pages 151-63

concerning their invention, can be found in Brewster (1856), Clay (1928), Gill (1969) and Maude (1978).

61 The two views have a much longer history than the stereoscope. Fusion theories can be traced back to Kepler, Aguilonious and Descartes in the seventeenth century; suppression notions were proposed in the sixteenth century by Porta and were developed later by du Tour and Gall. Historical treatments of binocular vision can be found in Boring (1942) and Gulick and Lawson (1976).

62 Eye dominance can be measured in many different ways, often with different results (see Porac and Coren, 1976). The type of eye dominance referred to here is usually called sensory or rivalry dominance.

63 Excellent examples of such stereoscopic depth effects can be found in Julesz (1971, 1978) and Frisby (1979). Julesz has developed a method for producing matrices of random dots which appear flat and meaningless when viewed by either eye alone, but within which parts appear in depth when combined binocularly. This is achieved by displacing some parts of the random dot patterns in each eye relative to one another.

64 See Breese (1899), Campbell and Howell (1972) and Wade (1975).

Chapter 2 Geometrical illusions

1 Purkinje (1823, 1825) wrote two monographs on subjective visual phenomena, such as after-images, entoptic phenomena, direct and indirect vision and a variety of distortions produced by viewing regular geometrical patterns. Purkinje was influenced initially by Goethe, and adopted the latter's phenomenological method. The range of phenomena observed by Purkinje and the clarity of his interpretations are awesome. As a consequence of his observational skills he gained access to one of the first achromatic microscopes: the success of his microscopy is attested by the various anatomical structures bearing his name. One of the best, and earliest, considerations of his work in English can be found in an anonymous article (almost certainly by Charles Wheatstone) published in the *Journal of the Royal Institution* (C.W., 1830). Other summaries of Purkinje's work can be found in Baly's translation of Müller's Handbook (Müller, 1842) and Helmholtz (1924).

2 Oppel (1855).

3 Necker (1832).

4 Many attempts at classifying illusions have been made in the various monographs addressed to them. One of the best discussions can be found in Boring (1942). Other books concerned with illusions are by Coren and Girgus (1978), Luckiesh (1922), Robinson (1972), Sully (1881) and Tolansky (1964). More general approaches to the relationship between illusions and art can be found in Thurston and Carraher (1966), Gregory and Gombrich

Notes to pages 163-89

(1973) and Lammers (1977).
5 Robinson's (1972) book provides a host of fascinating detail concerning research on visual illusions, defined more broadly than geometrical optical illusions.
6 Helmholtz (1925, p. 193) pitted the orientation of vertical and horizontal lines against a square framework to modify its apparent shape.
7 This is called Wundt's area illusion.
8 Georgeson (1973). Howard (1982) refers to this effect as tilt contrast.
9 Helmholtz (1924, vol. 2, p. 187).
10 This illusion has been called by many names like the displaced checkerboard pattern (Münsterberg, 1897), the kindergarten patterns (Pierce, 1898), and more recently the café-wall illusion (Gregory, 1973). Here it will be referred to as the Münsterberg illusion.
11 Fraser (1908).
12 Fraser (1908); see also Lammers (1977) for some interesting variations.
13 See Carr (1935), Judd (1905) and Wundt (1898).
14 Pritchard (1958); Evans and Marsden (1966).
15 See Alpern (1972) and Carpenter (1977).
16 Festinger, White and Allyn (1968); Virsu (1971).
17 See note 49 in Chapter 1. Hubel and Wiesel have summarized much of their own work in the 1977 Ferrier lecture delivered to the Royal Society (1977). In 1981 they shared the Nobel Prize for Medicine.
18 See Blakemore (1973), Blakemore, Carpenter and Georgeson (1970).
19 See Frisby (1979).
20 Gregory (1973).
21 These are often called misapplied constancy-scaling theories, because of their reliance on ideas common to the perceptual constancies. This approach has been advanced, with different emphases, by Thiéry (1896), Tausch (1954) and Gregory (1963).
22 The collection of essays in Epstein (1977) provides a sound introduction to the perceptual constancies.
23 See Hochberg (1971).
24 See Day (1972) and Gillam (1980).
25 See Coren and Girgus (1978).
26 See Hochberg (1971).
27 See Table 5.1 in Coren and Girgus (1978, p. 97).
28 See Robinson (1972, pp. 109-13).
29 See Pollack (1970) and Pollack and Silvar (1967).
30 Coren and Girgus (1978) have suggested methods by which the putative components involved in illusions can be distinguished.
31 Necker (1832) considered that the reversals were due to changes in the distinctiveness of the figure during observation. Presumably he was referring to changes in clarity associated with accommo-

dative shifts. The first serious discussion of Necker's phenomenon, by Wheatstone (1838), rejected this interpretation and suggested, in its stead, a 'cognitive' one — the figure seen corresponds to the solid figure inferred to be present. Wheatstone noted that the reversals were easier to obtain with one eye, and that they occurred when the eyes were fixed as steadily as possible on the figure.

32 Evans and Marsden (1966), Pritchard (1958).
33 See Hochberg's (1970) provocative essay.
34 The notion of satiation has been developed by Gestalt psychologists initially to account for figural after-effects (Köhler and Wallach, 1944), but it has since been used more widely (see Hochberg, 1971, Köhler and Fishback, 1950).
35 Many examples of distorted or impossible drawings can be found in artistic works (see, for example, Hogarth's works in Ireland and Nichols, 1883). Their psychological importance was appreciated by Penrose and Penrose (1958).
36 See Ware and Kennedy (1977).
37 See Gregory (1970).
38 Escher has also produced some of the finest examples of figure-ground reversal. Fortunately, reproductions of his work are readily available (see Escher, 1972; Escher and Locher, 1971; Ernst, 1976). For an analysis of Escher's use of the impossible triangle motif, see Draper (1978). Teuber (1974) argues that the inspiration for Escher's early graphic works derived from perceptual experiments by the Gestalt psychologists.

Chapter 3 Op-tical illusions

1 See Ponzo (1912) and Robinson (1972).
2 This possibility was raised by Robinson (1972).
3 See Moulden and Renshaw (1979) for a detailed examination of the determinants of the Münsterberg illusion.
4 See Gillam (1979).
5 Reproduction of Duchamp's rotoreliefs can be found in Barrett (1970). For further discussion of such rotating patterns see Duncan (1975), Fineman (1981) and Sekuler and Levinson (1977).
6 Early work on the stereokinetic depth effect was conducted by Musatti (1929), Metzger (1953) and Wallach and O'Connell (1953). A review of depth phenomena produced by motion is given by Braunstein (1976) and by Musatti (1975).

Bibliography

Airy, H. (1870), 'On a distinct form of transient hemiopsia', *Philosophical Transactions of the Royal Society, 160*, 247-64.
Alpern, M. (1972), 'Effector mechanisms in vision', in J.W. Kling and L.A. Riggs (eds), *Woodworth and Schlosberg's Experimental Psychology*, Methuen, London.
Ames, A., Proctor, C.A. and Ames, B. (1922), 'Vision and the technique of art', *Proceedings of the American Academy of Arts and Sciences, 58*, 3-47.
Arnheim, R. (1954), *Art and Visual Perception*, University of California Press, Berkeley.
Arnulf, A. and Dupuy, O. (1960), 'Contribution à l'étude des microfluctuations d'accommodation de l'oeil', *Revue d'Optique, Théorique et Instrumentale, 39*, 195-208.
Attneave, F. (1954), 'Some informational aspects of visual perception', *Psychological Review, 61*, 183-93.
Barrett, C. (1970), *Op Art*, Studio Vista, London.
Barrett, C. (1971), *An Introduction to Optical Art*, Studio Vista, London.
Baumgartner, G. (1960), 'Indirekte Grossenbestimmung der receptiven Felder der Retina beim Menschen mittels der Hermannschen Gittertäuschung', *Pflügers Archiv fur die Gestamte Physiologie des Menschen und der Tiere, 272*, 21-2.
Beardslee, D.C. and Wertheimer, M. (1958), *Readings in Perception*, Van Nostrand, London.
Békésy, G. von (1967), *Sensory Inhibition*, Princeton University Press, New Jersey.
Besant, A. and Leadbeater, C.W. (1905), *Thought-Forms*, Theosophical Publishing Society, London.
Blakemore, C. (1973), 'The baffled brain', in R.L. Gregory and E.H. Gombrich (eds) (1973), pp. 9-47.
Blakemore, C., Carpenter, R.H.S. and Georgeson, M.A. (1970), 'Lateral inhibition between orientation detectors in the human visual system', *Nature, 228*, 37-9.

Bibliography

Boring, E.G. (1942), *Sensation and Perception in the History of Experimental Psychology*, Appleton-Century-Crofts, New York.

Boynton, R.M. (1979), *Human Color Vision*, Holt, Rinehart & Winston, New York.

Braddick, O., Campbell, F.W. and Atkinson, J. (1978), 'Channels in vision: Basic aspects', in R. Held, H.W. Leibowitz, and H.-L. Teuber (eds), *Handbook of Sensory Physiology. Perception*, vol. 8, Springer, New York.

Braunstein, M.L. (1976), *Depth Perception through Motion*, Academic Press, London.

Breese, B.B. (1899), 'On inhibition', *Psychological Monographs, 3* (1), 1-65.

Brewster, D. (1825), 'On some remarkable affections of the retina as exhibited in its insensibility to indirect impressions, and to the impressions of attenuated light', *Edinburgh Journal of Science, 3*, 288-93.

Brewster, Sir D. (1844a), 'A notice explaining the cause of an optical phenomenon observed by the Rev. W. Selwyn', *Report of the British Association for the Advancement of Science: Transactions of the Sections*, p. 8.

Brewster, Sir D. (1844b), 'On the same subject', *Report of the British Association for the Advancement of Science: Transactions of the Sections*, p. 10.

Brewster, Sir D. (1856), *The Stereoscope, its History, Theory and Construction*, Murray, London.

Brigner, W.L. and Gallagher, M.B. (1974), 'Subjective contour: apparent depth or simultaneous brightness contrast?', *Perceptual and Motor Skills, 38*, 1047-53.

Brown, C.R., and Gebhard, J.W. (1948), 'Visual field articulation in the absence of spatial stimulus gradients', *Journal of Experimental Psychology, 38*, 188-200.

Brown, J.L. (1965), 'Afterimages', in C.H. Graham (ed.), *Vision and Visual Perception*, Wiley, New York, pp. 479-503.

Campbell, F.W. (1974), 'The transmission of spatial information through the visual system', in F.O. Schmitt and F.G. Worden (eds), *The Neurosciences: Third Study Program*, MIT Press, London, pp. 95-103.

Campbell, F.W. and Howell, E.R. (1972), 'Monocular alternation: a method for the investigation of pattern vision', *Journal of Physiology, 225*, 19-21 P.

Campbell, F.W. and Robson, J.G. (1958), 'Moving visual images produced by regular stationary patterns', *Nature, 181*, 362.

Campbell, F.W., Westheimer, G. and Robson, J.G. (1959), 'Fluctuations in accommodation under steady viewing conditions', *Journal of Physiology, 145*, 257-62.

Carpenter, R.H.S. (1977), *Movements of the Eyes*, Pion, London.

Carr, H.A. (1935), *An Introduction to Space Perception*, Longmans, New York.

Clay, R.S. (1928), 'The stereoscope', *Transactions of the Optical*

Society, 29, 149-66.
Cohen, J. and Gordon, D.A. (1949), 'The Prevost-Fechner-Benham subjective colors', *Psychological Bulletin, 46*, 97-133.
Compton, M. (1974), *Optical and Kinetic Art*, Tate Gallery, London.
Coren, S. (1972), 'Subjective contours and apparent depth', *Psychological Bulletin, 79*, 359-67.
Coren, S. and Girgus, J. (1978), *Seeing is Deceiving: the Psychology of Visual Illusions*, Erlbaum, Hillsdale, New Jersey.
Davson, H. (1972), *Physiology of the Eye*, 3rd edn, Churchill-Livingstone, London.
Day, R.H. (1972), 'Visual spatial illusions: a general explanation', *Science, 175*, 1335-40.
Ditchburn, D.W. (1973), *Eye Movements and Visual Perception*, Oxford University Press, London.
Draper, S.W. (1978), 'The Penrose triangle and a family of related figures', *Perception, 7*, 283-96.
Duke-Elder, Sir S. (1968), *System of Ophthalmology. The Physiology of the Eye and of Vision*, vol. 4, Henry Kimpton, London.
Duke-Elder, Sir S. (1970), *System of Ophthalmology. Ophthalmic Optics and Refraction*, vol. 5, Henry Kimpton, London.
Duncan, F.S. (1975), 'Kinetic art: on my psychokinematic objects', *Leonardo, 8*, 97-101.
Ellis, W.H. (1938), *Source Book of Gestalt Psychology*, Routledge & Kegan Paul, London.
Enroth-Cugell, C. and Robson, J.G. (1966), 'The contrast sensitivity of retinal ganglion cells of the cat', *Journal of Physiology, 187*, 517-52.
Epstein, W. (1977), *Stability and Constancy in Visual Perception*, Wiley, London.
Erb, M.B. and Dallenbach, K.M. (1939), ' "Subjective" colors from line patterns', *American Journal of Psychology, 52*, 227-41.
Ernst, B. (1976), *The Magic Mirror of M.C. Escher*, Ballantine, New York.
Escher, M.C. (1972), *The Graphic Works of M.C. Escher*, Pan/Ballantine, London.
Escher, M.C. and Locher, J.L. (1971), *The World of M.C. Escher*, Abrams, New York.
Evans, C.R. and Marsden, R.P. (1966), 'A study of the effect of perfect retinal stabilization on some well-known visual illusions, using the after-image as a method of compensating for eye movements', *British Journal of Physiological Optics, 23*, 242-8.
Exhibition Catalogue (1978), *An Exhibition of Venezuelan Art*, The Artists Market Association Gallery, London, July.
Festinger, L., White, C.W. and Allyn, M.R. (1968), 'Eye movements and decrement in the Müller-Lyer illusion', *Perception and Psychophysics, 3*, 376-82.
Fineman, M. (1981), *The Inquisitive Eye*, Oxford University Press.
Fraser, J. (1908), 'A new visual illusion of direction', *British Journal of Psychology, 2*, 307-20.
Frisby, J.P. (1979), *Seeing*, Oxford University Press, London.

Bibliography

Georgeson, M.A. (1973), 'Spatial frequency selectivity of a tilt illusion', *Nature, 245*, 43-5.
Georgeson, M.A. (1976a), 'Antagonism between channels for pattern and movement in human vision', *Nature, 259*, 413-15.
Georgeson, M.A. (1976b), 'Psychophysical hallucinations of orientation and spatial frequency', *Perception, 5*, 99-111.
Gibson, J.J. (1950), *The Perception of the Visual World*, Houghton Mifflin, Boston.
Gibson, J.J. (1966), *The Senses Considered as Perceptual Systems*, Houghton Mifflin, Boston.
Gibson, J.J. (1979), *The Ecological Approach to Visual Perception*, Houghton Mifflin, Boston.
Gill, A.T. (1969), 'Early stereoscopes', *The Photographic Journal, 109*, 546-59, 606-14, 641-51.
Gillam, B. (1979), 'Even a possible figure can look impossible!', *Perception, 8*, 229-32.
Gillam, B. (1980), 'Geometrical illusions', *Scientific American, 242*(1), 86-95.
Gombrich, E.H. (1959), *Art and Illusion*, Phaidon, London.
Gottschaldt, K. (1926), 'Über den Einfluss der Erfahrung auf die Wahrnehmung von Figuren', 1, *Psychologische Forschung, 8*, 261-317.
Gregory, R.L. (1963), 'Distortion of visual space as inappropriate constancy scaling', *Nature, 199*, 678-80.
Gregory, R.L. (1970), *The Intelligent Eye*, Weidenfeld and Nicolson, London.
Gregory, R.L. (1972), 'Cognitive contours', *Nature, 238*, 51-2.
Gregory, R.L. (1973), 'The confounded eye', in R.L. Gregory and E.H. Gombrich (eds) (1973), pp. 49-95.
Gregory, R.L. and Gombrich, E.H. (eds) (1973), *Illusion in Nature and Art*, Duckworth, London.
Gregory, R.L. and Heard, P. (1979), 'Border locking and the café wall illusion', *Perception, 8*, 365-80.
Grünau, M.W. von (1975), 'The "fluttering heart" and spatio-temporal characteristics of color processing', 1, *Vision Research, 15*, 431-6.
Guild, J. (1956), *The Interference Systems of Crossed Diffraction Gratings: Theory of Moiré Fringes*, Oxford University Press, London.
Gulick, W.L. and Lawson, R.B. (1976), *Human Stereopsis. A Psychophysical Analysis*, Oxford University Press, New York.
Hebb, D.O. (1949), *Organization of Behavior*, Wiley, New York.
Held, R. and Richards, W. (1972), *Perception: Mechanisms and Models*, Freeman, San Francisco.
Held, R. and Richards, W. (1976), *Recent Progress in Perception*, Freeman, San Francisco.
Helmholtz, H. von (1856), *Handbuch der physiologischen Optik*, vol. 1, Voss, Leipzig.
Helmholtz, H. von (1881), *Popular Lectures on Scientific Subjects*, 1st series, 2nd edn, translated by E. Atkinson, Longmans, London.

Helmholtz, H. von (1924), *Physiological Optics*, vols 1 and 2, English translation from the 3rd German edn by J.P.C. Southall, The Optical Society of America, Washington.

Helmholtz, H. von (1925), *Physiological Optics*, vol. 3, English translation from the 3rd German edn by J.P.C. Southall, The Optical Society of America, Washington.

Henle, M. (1961), *Documents of Gestalt Psychology*, University of California Press, Berkeley.

Hering, E. (1878), *Zur Lehre vom Lichtsinne*, Gerold, Wien.

Hermann, L. (1870), 'Eine Erscheinung simultanen Contrastes', *Pflügers Archiv für die Gesamte Physiologie des Menschen und der Tiere, 3*, 13-15.

Hochberg, J. (1970), 'In the mind's eye', in R.N. Haber (ed.), *Contemporary Theory and Research in Visual Perception*, Holt, Rinehart & Winston, London, pp. 309-31.

Hochberg, J. (1971), 'Perception I and II', in J.W. Kling and L.A. Riggs (eds), *Woodworth and Schlosberg's Experimental Psychology*, Methuen, London, pp. 395-550.

Hochberg, J. (1974), 'Organization and the Gestalt tradition', in E.C. Carterette and M.P. Friedman (eds), *Handbook of Perception. Historical and Philosophical Roots of Perception*, vol. 1, Academic Press, London, pp. 179-210.

Hohmann, A. and Malsburg, C. von der (1978), 'McCullough effect and eye optics', *Perception, 7*, 551-5.

Howard, I.P. (1982), *Human Visual Orientation*, Wiley, Chichester.

Hubel, D.H. and Wiesel, T.N. (1977), 'Ferrier Lecture: functional architecture of macaque monkey visual cortex', *Proceedings of the Royal Society of London, Series B, 198*, 1-59.

Hubel, D.H. and Wiesel, T.N. (1979), 'Brain mechanisms of vision', *Scientific American, 241* (3), 150-62.

Hurvich, L.M. (1981), *Color Vision*, Sinnauer Associates, Sunderland, Mass.

Ireland, J. and Nichols, J. (1883), *Hogarth's Works*, 1st, 2nd and 3rd series, Oliphant, Anderson & Ferrier, Edinburgh.

Itten, J. (1961), *The Art of Color*, Reinhold, New York.

Judd, C.H. (1905), 'The Müller-Lyer illusion', *Psychological Monographs, 7*, 55-81.

Julesz, B. (1971), *The Foundations of Cyclopean Perception*, University of Chicago Press.

Julesz, B. (1978), 'Global stereopsis: cognitive phenomena in stereoscopic depth perception', in R. Held, H.W. Leibowitz, and H.-L. Teuber (eds), *Handbook of Sensory Physiology. Perception*, vol. 8 Springer, New York, pp. 215-56.

Jung, R. (1971), 'Kontrastsehen, Konturbetonung, und Künstlerzeichnung', *Studium Generale, 24*, 1536-65.

Jung, R. (1973), 'Visual perception and neurophysiology', in R. Jung (ed.), *Handbook of Sensory Physiology. Central Processing of Visual Information*, vol. 7/3, part A, Springer, New York, pp. 1-152.

Jung, R. (1975), 'Contrast, contour and structure in visual physiology and pictorial representation', in *Die Spannweite des Humanes*, Deutsche Unesco Kommission, Köln Verlag Dokumentation, München, pp. 226-30.

Jung, R. and Spillmann, L. (1970), 'Receptive field estimation and perceptual integration in human vision', in F.A. Young and D.B. Lindsay (eds), *Early Experience and Visual Information Processing in Perceptual and Reading Disorders*, National Academy of Sciences, Washington, pp. 181-97.

Kandinsky, W. (1947), *Point and Line to Plane*, translated by H. Dearstyne and H. Rebay, Guggenheim Foundation, New York.

Kanizsa, G. (1976), 'Subjective contours', *Scientific American, 234*(4), 48-52.

Kanizsa, G. (1979), *Organization in Vision*, Praeger, New York.

Kaufman, L. (1974), *Sight and Mind*, Oxford University Press, London.

Koffka, K. (1935), *Principles of Gestalt Psychology*, Harcourt Brace, New York.

Köhler, W. (1929), *Gestalt Psychology*, Horace Liveright, New York.

Köhler, W. (1940), *Dynamics in Psychology*, Faber & Faber, London.

Köhler, W. and Fishback, J. (1950), 'The destruction of the Müller-Lyer illusion in repeated trials. I and II', *Journal of Experimental Psychology, 40*, 267-81, 398-410.

Köhler, W. and Wallach, H. (1944), 'Figural after-effect: an investigation of visual processes', *Proceedings of the American Philosophical Society, 88*, 269-357.

Krantz, S. (1974), *Science and Technology in the Arts*, Van Nostrand, London.

Kubovy, M. and Pomerantz, J.R. (eds) (1981), *Perceptual Organization*, Erlbaum, Hillsdale, New Jersey.

Lammers, E. (1977), *Illusions*, Thames & Hudson, London.

Lancaster, J. (1973), *Introducing Op Art*, Batsford, London.

Lavin, E. and Costall, A. (1978), 'Detection thresholds of the Hermann grid illusion', *Vision Research, 18*, 1061-2.

Lindsay, P.H. and Norman, D.A. (1972), *Human Information Processing*, Academic Press, London.

Lippard, L. (1967), 'Perverse perspectives', *Art International, 11*, 28-33.

Lucie-Smith, E. (1969), *Movements in Art since 1945*, Thames & Hudson, London.

Luckiesh, M. (1922), *Visual Illusions*, Constable, London.

McCullough, C. (1965), 'Color adaptation of edge-detectors in the human visual system', *Science, 149*, 1115-16.

MacKay, D.M. (1957), 'Moving visual images produced by regular stationary patterns', *Nature, 180*, 849-50.

MacKinnon, G.E., Forde, J. and Piggins, D.J. (1969), 'Stabilized images, steadily fixated figures and prolonged after-images', *Canadian Journal of Psychology, 23*, 184-95.

Marr, D. (1976), 'Early processing of visual information', *Philosophical Transactions of the Royal Society, Series B, 275*, 483-524.

Marr, D. and Nishihara, H.K. (1978), 'Visual information processing:

Artificial intelligence and the sensorium of sight', *Technology Review, 81,* 28-49.
Marx, E. (1973), *The Contrast of Colors,* Van Nostrand-Reinhold, New York.
Maude, N. (1978), 'Stereo photography, its inception, rise and fall', *British Journal of Photography,* 140-8.
Metzger, W. (1953), *Gesetze des Sehens,* Waldemar Kramer, Frankfurt.
Millodot, M. (1968), 'Influence of accommodation on the viewing of an optical illusion', *Quarterly Journal of Experimental Psychology,* 20, 329-35.
Mollon, J.D. (1979), 'The theory of colour vision', in K. Connolly (ed.), *Psychology Survey, no. 2,* Allen & Unwin, London, pp. 128-50.
Mollon, J.D. (1982), 'Color vision', *Annual Review of Psychology, 33,* 41-85.
Moulden, B. and Renshaw, J. (1979), 'The Münsterberg illusion and "irradiation" ', *Perception, 8,* 275-301.
Müller, J. (1842), *Elements of Physiology,* vol. 2, English translation by W. Baly, Taylor & Walton, London.
Münsterberg, H. (1897), 'Die verschobene Schachbrettfigur', *Zeitschrift für Psychologie, 15,* 184-8.
Musatti, C.L. (1929), 'Sui fenomeni stereocinetici', *Archivio Italiano di Psicologia, 3,* 105-20.
Musatti, C.L. (1975), 'Stereokinetic phenomena and their interpretation', in G.B. Flores d'Arcais (ed.), *Studies in Perception: Festschrift for Fabio Metelli,* Aldo Martello-Giunti, Milan.
Necker, L. (1832), 'Observations on some remarkable phenomena seen in Switzerland: and on an optical phenomenon which occurs when viewing a figure of a crystal or geometrical solid', *London and Edinburgh Philosophical Magazine and Journal of Science,* 1, 329-37.
Oatley, K. (1978), *Perceptions and Representations,* Methuen, London.
Oppel, J.J. (1855), 'Über geometrisch-optische Täuschungen', *Jahresbericht des Frankfurter Vereins,* 37-47.
Oster, G. (1964), *The Science of Moiré Patterns,* Edmund Scientific, Barrington, New Jersey.
Oster, G. (1965), 'Optical Art', *Optica Acta,* 4, 1359-69.
Oster, G. (1974), Interview in *Science and Technology in the Arts,* S. Krantz (ed.) (1974), pp. 127-8.
Oster, G. and Nishijima, Y. (1963), 'Moiré patterns', *Scientific American, 208*(5), 54-63.
Parola, R. (1969), *Optical Art,* Reinhold, London.
Penrose, L.S. and Penrose, R. (1958), 'Impossible objects: a special type of illusion', *British Journal of Psychology, 49,* 31-3.
Pierce, A.H. (1898), 'The illusions of the kindergarten patterns', *Psychological Review, 5,* 233-53.
Pierce, A.H. (1901), *Studies in Auditory and Visual Space Perception,* Longmans, Green, New York.
Pirenne, M.H. (1970), *Optics, Painting, and Photography,* Cambridge University Press.

Bibliography

Pollack, R.H. (1970), 'Müller-Lyer illusion: effect of age, lightness, contrast and hue', *Science, 170*, 93-5.

Pollack, R.H. and Silvar, S.D. (1967), 'Magnitude of the Müller-Lyer illusion in children as a function of pigmentation of the fundus oculi', *Psychonomic Science, 8*, 83-4.

Ponzo, M. (1912), 'Rapports de contraste angulaire et l'appréciation de grandeur des astres à l'horizon', *Archives Italiennes de Biologie, 58*, 327-9.

Popper, F. (1968), *Origins and Development of Kinetic Art*, Studio Vista, London.

Porac, C. and Coren, S. (1976), 'The dominant eye', *Psychological Bulletin, 83*, 880-97.

Pratt, F. (1979), 'The contribution of colour to three-dimensional ambiguities in paintings and drawings', *Perception, 8*, 157-73.

Pritchard, R.M. (1958), 'Visual illusions viewed as stabilized retinal images', *Quarterly Journal of Experimental Psychology, 10*, 77-81.

Pritchard, R.M. (1961), 'Stabilized images on the retina', *Scientific American, 204*, 72-8.

Purkinje, J. (1823), *Beobachtungen und Versuche zur Physiologie der Sinne: Beiträge zur Kenntniss des Sehens in subjektiver Hinsicht*, vol. 1, Calve, Prague.

Purkinje, J. (1825), *Beobachtungen und Versuche zur Physiologie der Sinne: Neue Beiträge zur Kenntniss des Sehens in subjektiver Hinsicht*, vol. 2, Reimer, Berlin.

Ratliff, F. (1965), *Mach Bands: Quantitative Studies on Neural Networks in the Retina*, Holden-Day, San Francisco.

Rayleigh, Lord (1878), 'On the manufacture and theory of diffraction gratings', *The London, Edinburgh and Dublin Philosophical Magazine and Journal of Science, 47*, 81-93.

Richards, W. (1971), 'The fortification illusions of migraines', *Scientific American, 224*(5), 88-96.

Richardson, T. and Stangos, N. (1974), *Concepts of Modern Art*, Penguin Books, Harmondsworth, Middlesex.

Riley, B. (1978), *Works 1959-78*, The British Council, London.

Ripps, H. and Weale, R.A. (1976), 'A sensation of visual flutter experienced after one had looked at parallel lines', in H. Davson (ed.), *The Eye. Visual Functions in Man*, vol. 2A, Academic Press, London, p. 143.

Robertson, B. (1971), 'Introduction and biographical note', in *Bridget Riley, Paintings and Drawings 1951-71*, Hayward Gallery, London.

Robinson, J.O. (1972), *The Psychology of Visual Illusion*, Hutchinson, London.

Rubin, E. (1915), *Synsoplevede Figurer*, Gyldendalske, Copenhagen.

de Sausmarez, M. (1970), *Bridget Riley*, Studio Vista, London.

Schumann, F. (1900), 'Beiträge zur Analyse der Gesichtswahrmehmungen: Einige Beobachtungen über die Zusammenfassung von Gesichtseindrücken zu Einheiten', *Zeitschrift für Psychologie, 23*, 1-32.

Seitz, W.C. (1966), *The Responsive Eye*, Museum of Modern Art, New York.

Sekuler, R. (1974), 'Spatial vision', *Annual Review of Psychology, 25*, 195-232.
Sekuler, R. and Levinson, E. (1977), 'The perception of moving targets', *Scientific American, 236*(1), 60-72.
Simplicius (1973), 'Unsung Heroes – I: J.-B. Moiré', in R.L. Weber (1973), pp. 199-200.
Soto, J.R. (1969), 'Catalogue for exhibition "Soto" ', Marlborough-Gerson Gallery, New York.
Spillmann, L. (1971), 'Foveal receptive fields in the human visual system measured with simultaneous contrast in grids and bars', *Pflügers Archiv für die Gesamte Physiologie des Menschen und der Tiere, 326*, 281-99.
Stanley, G. and Hoffman, W.C. (1976), 'Orientation-specific color effects without adaptation', *Bulletin of the Psychonomic Society, 7*, 513-14.
Stromeyer, C.F. (1978), 'Form-color aftereffects in human vision', in R. Held, H.W. Leibowitz and H.-L. Teuber (eds), *Handbook of Sensory Physiology. Perception*, vol. 8, Springer, New York, pp. 97-142.
Sully, J. (1881), *Illusions*, Kegan Paul, London.
Tausch, R. (1954), 'Optische Täuschungen ab artifizielle Effekte der Gestaltungsprocesse von Grössen und Formenkonstanz in der natürlichen Raumwahrnehmung', *Psychologische Forschung, 24*, 299-348.
Teuber, M.L. (1974), 'Sources of ambiguity in the prints of Maurits C. Escher', *Scientific American, 231* (1), 90-104.
Thiéry, A. (1896), 'Über geometrisch-optische Täuschungen', *Philosophische Studien, 12*, 76-126.
Thompson, D (1971), 'Bridget Riley', *Studio International, 182* (935), 16-21.
Thurston, J.B. and Carraher, R.G. (1966), *Optical Illusions and the Visual Arts*, Van Nostrand-Reinhold, New York.
Tolansky, S. (1964), *Optical Illusions*, Pergamon Press, London.
Trevor-Roper, P. (1970), *The World Through Blunted Sight*, Thames & Hudson, London.
Troscianko, T. (1982), 'A stereoscopic presentation of the Hermann grid', *Vision Research, 22*, 485-9.
Uttal, W.R. (1978), *The Psychobiology of Mind*, Lawrence Erlbaum, Hillsdale, New Jersey.
Uttal, W.R. (1981), *A Taxonomy of Visual Processes*, Erlbaum, Hillsdale, New Jersey.
Vasarely, V. (1965), *Vasarely*, Editions Griffon, Neuchatel.
Vasarely, V. (1973), *Planetary Folklore*, Bruckmann, Munich.
Verheijen, F.J. (1961), 'A simple afterimage method demonstrating the involuntary multi-directional eye movements during fixation', *Optica Acta, 8*, 309-11.
Virsu, V. (1971), 'Tendencies to eye movement, and misperception of curvature, direction and length', *Perception and Psychophysics, 9*, 65-72.

Wade, N.J. (1975), 'Monocular and binocular rivalry between contours', *Perception, 4*, 85-95.
Wade, N.J. (1977a), 'A note on the discovery of subjective colours', *Vision Research, 17*, 671-2.
Wade, N.J. (1977b), 'Distortions and disappearances of geometrical patterns', *Perception, 6*, 407-33.
Wade, N.J. (1978a), 'Op art and visual perception', *Perception, 7*, 21-46.
Wade, N.J. (1978b), 'Why do patterned afterimages fluctuate in visibility?', *Psychological Bulletin, 85*, 338-52.
Wade, N.J. and Day, R.H. (1978), 'On the colors seen in achromatic patterns', *Perception and Psychophysics, 23*, 261-4.
Wallach, H. and O'Connell, D.N. (1953), 'The kinetic depth effect', *Journal of Experimental Psychology, 45*, 205-17.
Ware, C. and Kennedy, J.M. (1977), 'Illusory line linking solid rods', *Perception, 6*, 601-2.
Weale, R.A. (1968), *From Sight to Light*, Oliver & Boyd, Edinburgh.
Weber, R.L. (1973), *A Random Walk in Science*, Institute of Physics, London.
Weisstein, N. (1980), 'The joy of Fourier analysis', in C.S. Harris (ed.), *Visual Coding and Adaptability*, Erlbaum, Hillsdale, New Jersey, pp. 365-80.
Wertheimer, M. (1923), 'Untersuchungen zur Lehre von der Gestalt, II', *Psychologische Forschung, 4*, 301-50.
Wheatstone, C. (1827), 'Description of the kaleidophone, or phonic kaleidoscope: a new philosophical toy, for the illustration of several interesting and amusing acoustical and optical phenomena', *Quarterly Journal of Science, Literature and Arts, 23*, 344-51.
C.W. (1830), 'Contributions to the physiology of vision, no. I', *Journal of the Royal Institution, 1*, 107-17.
Wheatstone, C. (1838), 'Contributions to the physiology of vision – part the first. On some remarkable, and hitherto unobserved, phenomena of binocular vision', *Philosophical Transactions of the Royal Society, 128*, 371-94.
Wheatstone, C. (1844), 'On a singular effect of the juxtaposition of certain colours under particular circumstances', *Report of the British Association for the Advancement of Science: Transactions of the Sections*, p. 10.
Wilding, L. (1973), *Räumliche Irritationen: optische Interferenzen perspektivische Täuschungen*, Kölnische Kunstverein, Köln.
Wilding, L. (1976), *Stereoscopische Scheinräume, Objekte und Anaglyphen*, Stadtlische Kunsthalle, Düsseldorf.
Wilding, L. (1977), *Sehen und Wahrnehmen*, published personally, Hamburg.
Wolfe, J.M. and Owens, D.A. (1981), 'Is accommodation colorblind? Focusing chromatic contours', *Perception, 10* 53-62.
Wundt, W. (1898), 'Die geometrisch – optischen Täuschungen', *Abhandlungen der Sachsischen Akademie der Wissenschaften, 24*, 53-178.
Young, T. (1800), 'Outlines of experiments and enquiries respecting

sound and light', *Philosophical Transactions of the Royal Society*, *90*, 106-50.

Young, T. (1801), 'On the mechanism of the eye', *Philosophical Transactions of the Royal Society*, *91*, 23-88.

Index of names

Aguilonius, F., 274
Airy, H., 270, 277
Allyn, M.R., 275, 279
Alpern, M., 271, 275, 277
Ames, A., 269, 277
Ames, B., 269, 277
Arnheim, R., 266, 277
Arnulf, A., 268, 277
Atkinson, J., 273, 278
Attneave, F., 273, 277

Baly, W., 274, 283
Barrett, C., 265, 267, 272, 276, 277
Baumgartner, G., 272, 277
Beardslee, D.C., 265, 277
Békésy, G. von, 266, 277
Besant, A., 267, 277
Blakemore, C., 273, 275, 277
Boring, E.G., 274, 278
Boynton, R.M., 270, 278
Braddick, O., 273, 278
Braunstein, M.L., 276, 278
Breese, B.B., 274, 278
Brewster, D., 270, 271, 272, 273, 274, 278
Brigner, W.L., 273, 278
Brown, C.R., 270, 278
Brown, J.L., 270, 278

Campbell, F.W., 268, 273, 274, 278
Carpenter, R.H.S., 271, 275, 277, 278
Carr, H.A., 275, 278
Carraher, R.G., 274, 285
Clay, R.S., 274, 278
Cohen, J., 270, 279
Compton, M., 265, 267, 279
Coren, S., 274, 275, 279, 284

Costall, A., 272, 282

Dallenbach, K.M., 270, 279
Davson, H., 269, 279
Day, R.H., 269, 275, 279, 286
Descartes, R., 274
Ditchburn, D.W., 266, 279
Draper, S.W., 276, 279
Duchamp, M., 256, 271, 276
Duke-Elder, S., 268, 269, 279
Duncan, F.S., 276, 279
Dupuy, O., 268, 278

Ellis, W.H., 265, 266, 279
Enroth-Cugell, C., 267, 279
Epstein, W., 275, 279
Erb, M.B., 270, 279
Ernst, B., 276, 279
Escher, M.C., 191, 276, 279
Evans, C.R., 268, 275, 276, 279

Festinger, L., 275, 279
Fineman, M., 276, 279
Fishback, J., 276, 282
Forde, J., 268, 282
Fraser, J., 164, 165, 275, 279
Frisby, J.P., 272, 274, 275, 279

Gall, F.J., 274
Gallagher, M.B., 273, 278
Gebhard, J.W., 270, 278
Georgeson, M.A., 270, 275, 278, 280
Gibson, J.J., 273, 280
Gill, A.T., 274, 280
Gillam, B., 275, 276, 280
Girgus, J., 274, 275, 279

Index

Goethe, J.W., 274
Gombrich, E.H., 265, 274, 280
Gordon, D.A., 270, 279
Gottschaldt, K., 266, 280
Gregory, R.L., 186, 266, 274, 275, 276, 280
Grünau, M.W., von, 272, 280
Guild, J., 267, 280
Gulick, W.L., 274, 280

Heard, P., 280
Hebb, D.O., 273, 280
Held, R., 272, 280
Helmholtz, H. von, 76, 164, 268, 269, 270, 274, 275, 280, 281
Henle, M., 265, 281
Hering, E., 271, 272, 281
Hermann, L., 272, 281
Hochberg, J., 275, 276, 281
Hoffman, W.C., 268, 269, 285
Hogarth, W., 276
Hohmann, A., 269, 281
Howard, I.P., 275, 281
Howell, E.R., 274, 278
Hubel, D.H., 185, 272, 275, 281
Hurvich, L., 270, 271, 281

Ireland, J., 276, 281
Itten, J., 271, 281

Judd, C.H., 275, 281
Julesz, B., 267, 274, 281
Jung, R., 266-7, 272, 281, 282

Kandinsky, W., 266, 282
Kanizsa, G., 265, 273, 282
Kaufman, L., 270, 282
Kennedy, J.M., 276, 286
Kepler, J., 274
Koffka, K., 3, 265, 282
Köhler, W., 3, 265, 276, 282
Krantz, S., 267, 282
Kubovy, M., 265, 282

Lammers, E., 275, 282
Lancaster, J., 265, 282
Lavin, E., 272, 282
Lawson, R.B., 274, 280
Leadbeater, C.W., 267, 278
Levinson, E., 276, 285
Lindsay, P.H., 266, 282
Lippard, L., 266, 282
Locher, J.L., 276, 279
Lucie-Smith, E., 265, 282
Luckiesh, M., 274, 282

McCullough, C., 268, 282
Mach, E., 266
MacKay, D.M., 268, 270, 282
MacKinnon, G.E., 268, 282
Malsburg, C. von der, 269, 281
Marr, D., 273, 282
Marsden, R.P., 268, 275, 276, 279
Marx, E., 271, 283
Maude, N., 274, 283
Metzger, W., 276, 283
Millodot, M., 268, 283
Moiré, J.-B., 266
Mollon, J.D., 270, 283
Moulden, B., 276, 283
Müller, J., 274, 283
Münsterberg, H., 275, 283
Musatti, C., 276, 283

Necker, L.A., 162, 274, 275, 283
Nichols, J., 276, 281
Nishihara, H.K., 273, 282
Nishijima, Y., 266, 283
Norman, D., 266, 282

Oatley, K., 266, 283
O'Connell, D.N., 276, 286
Oppel, J.J., 162, 274, 283
Oster, G., 266, 283
Owens, D.A., 272, 286

Parola, R., 265, 283
Penrose, L.S., 191, 276, 283
Penrose, R., 191, 276, 283
Pierce, A.H., 270, 275, 283
Piggins, D., 268, 283
Pirenne, M.H., 268, 283
Pollack, R.H., 275, 284
Pomerantz, J.R., 265, 282
Ponzo, M., 199, 276, 284
Popper, F., 265, 284
Porac, C., 274, 284
Porta, J.B., 274
Pratt, F., 266, 284
Pritchard, R., 266, 268, 275, 276, 284
Proctor, C.A., 269, 278
Purkinje, J.E., 162, 270, 274, 284

Ratliff, F., 266, 284
Rayleigh, Lord, 37, 266, 267, 284
Renshaw, J., 276, 283
Richards, W., 265, 270, 272, 280, 284
Richardson, T., 265, 284
Riley, B., 78, 101, 266, 270, 271, 284
Ripps, H., 270, 284

289

Index

Robertson, B., 270, 284
Robinson, J.O., 163, 270, 272, 274, 275, 276, 284
Robson, J.G., 267, 268, 278, 279
Rubin, E., 4, 265, 284

Sausmarez, M. de, 270, 284
Schumann, F., 273, 284
Seitz, W.C., 265, 284
Sekuler, R., 273, 276, 285
Selwyn, W., 272
Silvar, S.D., 275, 284
Simplicius, 266, 285
Soto, J.-R., 38, 267, 285
Spillman, L., 272, 282, 285
Stangos, N., 265, 284
Stanley, G., 268, 269, 285
Stromeyer, C.F., 268, 269, 285
Sully, J., 274, 285

Tausch, R., 275, 285
Teuber, M.L., 276, 285
Thiéry, A., 275, 285
Thompson, D., 270, 285
Thurston, J.B., 274, 285
Tolansky, S., 274, 285
Tour, E.F. du, 274
Trevor-Roper, P., 268, 285

Troscianko, T., 272, 285

Uttal, W.R., 271, 285

Vasarely, V., 1, 107, 265, 266, 267, 273, 285
Verheijen, F.J., 271, 285
Virsu, V., 275, 285

Wade, N.J., 265, 269, 270, 271, 274, 286
Wallach, H., 276, 282, 286
Ware, C., 276, 286
Weale, R.A., 268, 270, 284, 286
Weber, R.L., 266, 286
Weisstein, N., 273, 286
Wertheimer, Max, 3, 265, 286
Wertheimer, Michael, 265, 278
Westheimer, G., 268, 278
Wheatstone, C., 267, 271, 273, 274, 276, 286
White, C.W., 275, 279
Wiesel, T.N., 185, 272, 275, 281
Wilding, L., 37, 267, 286
Wolfe, J.W., 272, 286
Wundt, W., 275, 286

Young, T., 267, 268, 286, 287

Index of subjects

Names in italics refer to illustrations.
Numbers in italics refer to the pages on which illustrations appear.

About Turn, *89*
accommodation, 73-4, 151
aesthetic appeal of designs, 8-9, 264
after-images, 2, 100-1, 190, 199-200, 268, 270
anaglyphs, 152-3, 273
apparent angle expansion, 185
apparent movement, 36, 73-5
apparent size and apparent distance, 186-7, 189
art appreciation, 2, 8
artificial pupil, 74, 268
Astigmat, *61*
astigmatism: axis of, 74-5; pattern distortions due to, 2, 73-6, 134; regular, 74, 76-7, 240; transient, 74-6, 268
attention, eye fixation and, 5

Bali Dancers, 75, *92*
Bather, *65*
Beaunis cubes, 189, *193*
binocular fusion and suppression, 151-2, 274
binocular rivalry, 3, 38, 151-4, 274
binocular vision, 3, 151

café-wall illusion, 275
checkerboard patterns, 3, 108-9
chromatic aberration, 76, 102, 269
Chrysanthemum, 74-5, *84*
closure, 6
cognitive approaches to perception, 5, 75, 266

colour assimilation, 102
colour-contingent after-effects, 268-9
colour contrast, 76, 102, 269, 271
colour mixing, 270-1
complementary colours, 100
constancy scaling, illusions and, 186-8, 199
contour orientation, astigmatism and, 73-6
contours: artistic use of, 5, 266; definition of, 133; in visual perception, 133, 273
contrast effects, *see* simultaneous contrast
convergence, 151
Curvaceous Border, *90*

depth impressions: ambiguity of, 75, 162, 189-90, 240; in checkerboard patterns, 108; in illusion figures, 186-7, 200; in moiré patterns, 37-8; in rotating patterns, 256, 276; stereoscopic, 151-4; and subjective contours, 133-5
devil's pitchfork, 190, *194*

Ehrenstein illusion, *172*, 200
embedded figures, 6-9
eternal staircase, 191, *195*
extent, illusions of, 184-8, 199
eye dominance, 152, 274
eye fixation, 4-5, 75, 101, 107, 134, 256
eye movements: figure reversals and,

291

Index

190; illusions and, 184-5; involuntary, 73, 77, 101, 268, 271; pattern disappearances and, 5; pattern distortions due to, 73, 268
eye movement tendencies, 185, 190
eye, as an optical instrument, 73, 76, 269

Facial Frequency, 99
figure-ground segregation, 2, 4-5, 7, 198, 240
fluttering hearts phenomenon, 102, 271-2
foreshortening, 186
Forfeit, 8, *34*
Fourier analysis, 108, 273
Fraser illusions, 154-5, *183*, 202

geometrical abstraction, 1-2
geometrically periodic patterns, 35-6, 38, 77, 267-8
Gestalt grouping principles, 3-9, 133, 135-6, 265
Gestalt psychology, 2-3, 265, 276
good continuation, 6, 8, 108, 133, 136
good figure, 6
gratings, 35, 37-8, 240, 267
grids, 3, 106-8; *see also* Hermann-Hering grid

haloes, after-images and, 101
harmonograph, 36, 267
Hering grid, 200
Hermann-Hering grid: eye movements and, 107; lateral inhibition in, 106; receptive field dimensions from, 107, 272-3; subjective contours and, 135

illusion figures: Delboeuf, *166*; Hering, *175*; Lipps, *169*, *175*; Luckiesh, *171*; Oppel-Kundt, *169*; Orbison, *170*, *173*, *174*; Oyama, *173*; Tolansky, *168*; Wundt, *172*, *176*
illusions: age changes and, 188; artists' and scientists' approaches to, 1, 161, 263-4; classification of, 163, 184, 274; cultural differences in, 188; geometrical optical, 161, 163-5; in other species, 188-9; practice effects on, 188; second order, 108; tactile, 188
illusions, theories of, 184-8, 275
illusory dots, 3, 106, 135; *see also* Hermann-Hering grid

image focussing, 73-4
impossible objects, 75, 162-3, 190-1, 240, 276
impossible triangle, 190, *195*
irradiation, in the Münsterberg illusion, 201-2
irradiation illusion, 164, *182*

kindergarten patterns, 275

lateral inhibition, 36, 102, 266-7
Lateral Interaction, 64
Legacy, 8, *33*
Linear Contrast, 61
luminance boundary, 133-4

Mach book, 189, *192*
Maltese cross, 134, 240
masking of forms by perceptual grouping, 8-9
migraine, 270
moiré fringes, *see* moiré patterns
moiré patterns: anaglyphs and, 153; binocular rivalry with, 38, 153; dynamic, 2, 36-7; irregularities in, 37; lateral inhibition and, 36, 267; line spacing effects on, 35-6, 108; mathematical description of, 35, 37, 266; in Op Art, 2, 266; simultaneous contrast in, 36, 109; stereoscopic depth perception with, 37-8, 153, 267; three-dimensional, 2, 36-8, 266-7; transparency method for producing, 37-8
monocular rivalry, 153-4
mosaics: perceptual grouping in, 3; seen in binocular rivalry, 152
Müller-Lyer illusion, *166*, 184, 186-8, 199
Münsterberg illusion, *176*, *182*, 201-2, 275-6

Necker cube, 162, 189-90, *192*, 240
neural inhibition, illusions and, 185-6
neurophysiology of vision, 106, 185, 263, 272

Op Art: binocular rivalry in, 154; classification of works, 2-3; definition of, 1-2; descriptive language for, 263; disturbing effects of, 77, 270; origins, 1, 265; phenomena involved in, 161
Op Art, 62
Op Artists, 1-3, 7, 77, 152, 263, 266

Op Eye, 38, *72*, 73
Op-position, 75, *96*
optical characteristics of the eye, 39, 74, 76, 268-9
optical distortions, 2, 73-8
op-tical illusions, 198-202
orientation: detectors, 185-6; illusions, 163-4, 184-6, 188, 199-201; perception of, 185-6, 201-2
Outward Facing, 150

pattern alternation, 153-4
pattern blurring: transient astigmatism and, 73-5, 134, 268; eye movements and, 73, 268
pattern-specific accommodation, 269
perceptual ambiguity, 4, 189-91, 240
perceptual constancy, 275; and illusions, 186-8; in reversing figures, 189
perceptual organization, 2-9; in abstract designs, 266
perspective, 161, 199
perspective cues: in illusions, 186-8; in outline drawings, 162, 189-91
perspective reversals, 162
pictorial puzzles, 8-9, 264
Playboy, 71, 73
Poggendorff illusion, *168*, 200
Ponzo illusion, *167*, 186, 199
profiles, 8, 35, 37, 133
proximity, 4, 6

random-dot stereograms, 153, 274
Raydons, 82
receptive fields, 106-7, 185, 272-3
Reflections, 75, 86
retinal disparity, 37-8, 151
reversing figures, 4, 189-90, 198, 240, 275-6
rotoreliefs, 256, 276
Rubin's vase/faces figure, 4, 9, 35, 37, 100, 133-5, 153, 201, 240
Rückstrahlung, 135, *144*

satiation, figure reversals and, 190, 276
Schröder staircase, 189, *193*, 240
See Nymphs, 91

similarity, 6
simultaneous colour contrast, 76, 269
simultaneous contrast, 2-3, 101-2, 105-6, 109, 134, 271
size constancy, 187
Snowfall, 107, *114*
Spatially Frequent, 98
stabilized retinal images, 5, 100, 184, 190, 265-6, 268, 271
stereokinetic effect, 198, 256, 276
stereoscope, 151, 273-4
stereoscopic depth perception, 3, 151-3, 274
streaming phenomenon, 77, 270
subjective colours, 76-7, 240, 269-70
subjective contours: changes in line orientation and, 135, 153; definition of, 3, 133; Gestalt grouping principles and, 133, 135-6; illusions with, 186, 200; physiological interpretation of, 134; produced by incomplete figures, 107, 133-5; shadow effects in, 135
Subjectively Contoured, 63
suppression, local and global, 152
symmetry, 6-7, 9

The Model, 75, *95*
tilt contrast, 275
tilt illusion, 164, *181*
Titchener illusion, *167*, 200
Topol, 149
Torson, 8, *32*
trigger features, 185

vertical-horizontal illusion, 163, *177*, *178*, *179*, 184, 186
visual art and visual science, 1-2, 9, 161, 256, 263, 266-7
visual direction, 151
visual resolution, 5, 73-4, 78
visual space, distortions of, 162

watered silk, 35
Wundt's area illusion, *180*, 275

Zöllner illusion, *170*, *171*, 200-1

293